THE
FOREVER DOG

Also by Dr. Karen Shaw Becker
and Rodney Habib

The Forever Dog

THE
FOREVER DOG
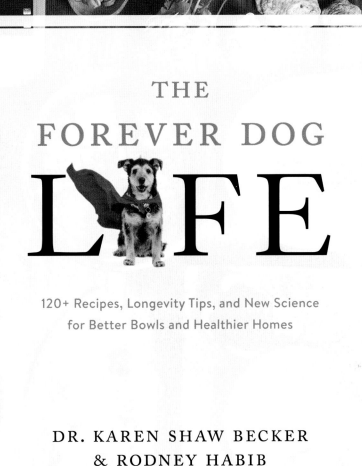
L**I**FE

120+ Recipes, Longevity Tips, and New Science
for Better Bowls and Healthier Homes

DR. KAREN SHAW BECKER
& RODNEY HABIB

with Sarah Durand

18 17

HARPER

An Imprint of HarperCollinsPublishers

To our moms, Jeannine and Salwa (Sally), and every mom around the world who wants their children to experience the life-changing benefits of growing up with animals and creating a culture of kindness by treating pets as important members of the family. And thank you for nourishing us well. Because of you, we know the power of healthy food that comes from the heart.

Contents

Authors' Note

Like its prequel, *The Forever Dog*, this book is heavily referenced with scientific studies, primary and secondary sources, and additional resources. Some of these studies used human subjects, but since pets' and humans' digestive tracts evolved at the same time—unless noted—what's good for us is likely good for them. *The Forever Dog Life* also includes over 120 recipes and household tips to promote your beloved companion's longevity and overall health and happiness. In the interest of keeping the pages and photos as user-friendly as possible, we have listed the nutritional analyses of the complete and balanced meals and all our citations and references on the book's website, www.foreverdog.com. As with *The Forever Dog*, hosting the source material at our book website also allows us to continually update our book's scientific backbone as it evolves and grows. Data changes, but your reading experience doesn't have to suffer for it. Instead, we want you to focus 100 percent on learning how to support, nurture, and love your Forever Dogs and Cats—today, tomorrow, and always.

Conqueiros BOBI'S BACKYARD

INTRODUCTION

In January 2023, we began to hear rumors about the existence of a dog who'd lived well into his twenties—and possibly beyond thirty. This Forever Dog was Bobi—a soft-coated, medium-sized brown-and-white *rafeiro* (meaning mongrel, mutt, or mixed-breed) from Conqueiros, a small village in west-central Portugal.

We immediately went on a mission to connect with him. Karen posted an on-line plea, begging people to contact us if anyone knew anything about Bobi. Within minutes, we received over a hundred comments, and within an hour, we were tagged thousands of times.

A few days later, Rodney's phone pinged with a message: "Hello Rodney, this is Leonel. Would you like to come to Portugal and meet Bobi?"

We booked our flight and hopped on a plane as quick as we could.

We found Bobi and his human companion, Leonel Costa, living in a house with a massive garden in the front and—during most years—chickens and rabbits in the backyard. Leonel's family grows much of the food they eat, including cabbages, potatoes, tomatoes, lettuce, cucumbers, parsley, and cilantro. They also visit the local farmers' market each week to pick up fresh fish. Bobi had always eaten home-made meals consisting of healthy human leftovers, including grilled *dourada* (gilt-head sea bream), cooked carrots, broc-coli, potatoes (dusted with salt), a chicken broth called *canja*, and a bit of *broa*, a Portuguese corn bread Leonel sprinkled with olive oil to make it easier for Bobi to swallow.

Right away, Bobi's diet brought to mind Darcy, a twenty-one-year-old tiny mixed-breed Forever Dog we'd met several years before. His parents had fed him home-cooked meals since he was seven years old, often consisting of fresh salmon, mussels, turmeric, and a splash of apple cider vinegar as a base. We also thought back to Maggie, a reportedly thirty-year-old kelpie from Australia who died in 2016 after a life spent consuming farm-fresh raw milk, oxtails, and healthy table scraps. These animals had one thing in common: human-grade, fresh, colorful, nutritious food that improved every single one of their biological processes.

Bobi had been born in a woodpile in the Costas' backyard shed, and he'd spent the bulk of his time outside. In his prime, Bobi loved to jump over the property walls and chase the mail carrier, but in his old age

he nibbled from the garden, took long walks through the fruit groves and forest close to their house—always saying hello to the neighborhood dogs along the way—slept outside, and lovingly interacted with his family every chance he got. This active existence was like Augie, the double-decade golden retriever whose dad told us she swam an hour a day throughout most of her life, as well as Bluey, the Australian cattle dog (born in 1910), who'd lived for twenty-nine years and five months. Bluey worked on a farm in Victoria, herding sheep and cattle for his family. Maggie ran three miles back and forth across her family's farm twice a day, seven days a week, for two decades. *That's over 87,000 miles of running in one lifetime.*

These Forever Dogs' owners didn't know that—according to the latest science—their simple, commonsense way of life offered their animals all the variables for exceptional health and longevity: a varied intake of nutrient-dense, minimally processed foods; daily exercise; minimal exposure to environmental chemicals and toxins; low stress; and rich social lives. These habits benefit humans—and their pets.

While there's no definitive test for determining the exact age of a living creature, scientists rely on DNA methylation and telomere testing to gain insights. Telomeres are the protective caps on chromosomes that shorten over time and can be used to approximate biologic age. Telomere testing had been completed prior to our arrival in Portugal, with results showing Bobi was between twenty-eight and thirty-two years old. But we were just as curious as the rest of the

Fatty Acids Help Hair Grow: From the first moment we met Bobi, one thing that struck us was his thick, shiny coat. Throughout his entire life, he consumed omega-3-rich foods, whose fatty acids promote hair growth by increasing the number of dermal papilla cells (DPC) and their associated proteins. Oily fish contain lots of the fatty acid docosahexaenoic acid, or DHA. The *dourada* it was!

world to double-check this, so we also collected DNA swabs on our visit, sending them for epigenetic clock testing at Dr. Enikő Kubinyi's lab in Hungary. Epigenetic clock swabs reveal DNA methylation patterns that provide an estimated biologic age, as compared to chronologic age (our birth year). If a biologic age is higher than the chronologic age, it suggests accelerated aging, while a lower biologic age may indicate a slower aging process. Bobi's DNA results were similar to the telomere test: his biologic age was between twenty-three and thirty-five. And despite all the media hoopla surrounding Bobi's possible status as the world's longest living dog on record, Leonel's neighbors said it best: this old dog had been around town for decades . . . clearly, he did *something* right.

We want to imbue this book with the same degree of love and care the Forever Pets we've described enjoyed throughout their long lives. Through a journey across the world, featuring different cultures and cuisines, we also aim to show how you, too, can strive to have a Forever Pet. While this book has "dog" in the title, it's intended for both dogs and cats. Indeed, *The Forever Dog Life* is about celebrating wholesome, nourishing food and creating a nontoxic home environment that provides families and *all* their pets an oasis for health and well-being.

The Forever Dog Life introduces the most nutrient-dense Forever Foods that will boost your pets' health, and it offers a multitude of feeding techniques, DIY tricks, research highlights, nutrition information, tools, and household and money-saving tips. Then we dive into recipes, from treats and toppers to complete and balanced meals your pet can enjoy daily. Many of these recipes incorporate our Forever Foods. Food is medicine, and this book will help you gain the confidence to do it right. But please note: This isn't a regular cookbook. In fact, this isn't really a cookbook at all (although most of the recipes are cookable, if you want). These are *recipes for life*!

Good health is built on more than nutritious food, however. Bored pets who lack sufficient exercise, social engagement, and enriching activities can suffer mentally, phys-

Seek Out Nature: There are now dozens of studies confirming *shinrin-yoku* ("forest bathing"), or spending time in nature or the woods, has numerous health benefits, including:

- Reduced blood pressure
- Lower stress
- Improved cardiovascular and metabolic health
- Weight loss

- Lower blood sugar levels
- Improved concentration and memory
- Lower rates of depression
- Higher energy levels
- Boosted immunity

ically, and emotionally. For instance, studies show that keeping your dog mentally engaged fights inflammation and benefits the immune system. In addition, the more enrichment you provide your pet, the more brain-derived neurotropic factor (BDNF) is produced, which keeps brain cells healthy and stimulates new brain cell growth. Throughout the book, we've sprinkled ideas and science to help you keep your animals entertained so that every cell in their bodies can flourish.

We live in incredibly stressful and toxic homes, yards, cities, and habitats, and these pressures hit our pets from all sides: with nutritional deficiencies, obesity, indoor and outdoor exposures, veterinary practices (de-sexing, annual vaccines, flea and tick chemical application, and drugs that disrupt the microbiome), and more. This book addresses all forms of stress, showing you how you can reduce the damaging effects of these variables. As guardians of animals that can't choose for themselves, we owe it to them to do all we can to help them live better and healthier. We'll show you how.

As you focus on food and the environment, the following LIFE strategy will help to ensure exceptional health and longevity. An animal's

L: Lifestyle
(Pets need love, enrichment, exercise, and good, proactive medical care.)

I: Ideal microbiome
(A robust ecosystem of intestinal microbes is key to building immunity, fighting disease, and facilitating healthy metabolic processes within the body.)

F: Food
(A diverse diet complete with fresh, whole, minimally processed foods is vital to an animal's longevity.)

E: Environment and Stress
(Our companions need "green" homes free of environmental contaminants, toxic personal care products, and foods that minimize stress on their body systems.)

immediate environment and the choices you make for them are what ultimately have the biggest impact on their well-being.

The first part of this book focuses on what the *body* needs, discussing the Forever Foods that maximize nutritional status, act as preventive medicine, and offer the cells, tissues, bones, organs, and more the opportunity to heal and rebalance. You can integrate these foods at your own pace, starting with treats, toppers, broths, stews, and teas, or jumping right into making nutritionally complete recipes (raw, cooked, baked, or Crock-Pot). The second half of the book shows you how to support your dog's health from the *outside* in: intentionally creating a safer and healthier environment around your animal. Addressing your pets' immediate living area is critical for managing epigenetic risks and DNA damage, which ultimately play into health and longevity or disease and degeneration.

According to the longevity experts we interviewed, 20 percent of health is genetic, and 80 percent is environmental. That means *the vast majority of your pet's long-term health is within your control. The Forever Dog Life* will make it easier (and likely less expensive) to do more to nourish our animals and keep pollutants out of their bloodstreams. We'll show you how to "swap up," exchanging a current lifestyle decision for a healthier one that allows you to move *up* the scale of nutrition and health. Every bite of fresher treats and foods means more consumption of health-promoting, microbiome-protecting bioactive substances, and each endocrine-disrupting household chemical cleaner that's replaced with a nontoxic DIY option reduces metabolic and environmental stress on your furries. A healthy life is made up of making one good decision at a time, over and over. Incorporating one, some, or all these beneficial changes is a step toward doing all you can to create a Forever Pet.

Your pet can enjoy a vibrant, lower-stress, wholesome life that you did your very best to extend. With the tools in this book, you, too, can raise a Forever Pet, meaning you have committed to creating a healthier, happier life for your animals—intentionally, with no regrets. Come into our kitchens and homes so that we can show you how.

How to Have a "Blue Zone" Pet: The term "Blue Zone" refers to geographic regions around the world where people live significantly longer, healthier lives, compared to global averages. Researchers have studied why these areas have unusually high concentrations of people over one hundred and have identified these characteristics: regular physical activity, a Mediterranean-type diet, strong social bonds, and a low-stress lifestyle. We'll show you how your pet's way of life can check all four of those boxes.

When Sarah, our awesome book collaborator, and her husband, Peter, picked up their first dog—a two-and-a-half-year-old shih tzu/poodle mix—from a rural shelter near their home, they just assumed he'd have hair. McGee was a mess of gray curls in his online pictures, with only a single canine extending up from his lower jaw as evidence that he was, in fact, a dog and not a dirty mop. But when the shelter staff walked him to their waiting room on adoption day, he was bald as an egg. "He had some mats, so we had to shave him," the staff member said. "Sorry he looks like a rat."

In his first month, McGee's coat grew in wiry and coarse. Soon, there was a patch of hair on his rear that was mottled, darker, and drier than the surrounding hair. The couple eliminated the kibble that his previous owner had been serving him and swapped up to sardines, knowing that fish's DHA would help his coat. They mixed the fish with pumpkin and avocado, understanding that their rich vitamin E content was excellent for dry skin and coarse hair. Soon his hair grew soft and shiny. The dark patch on his rear end faded and blended into a soft, manageable, and healthy coat.

We've seen transformations like these over and over, and every time it's still so satisfying; dull, dry hair is replaced with shiny, softer fur; bad breath and stinky poop diminish; and clearer eyes and ears emerge when fresh food replaces fast food. This is the power of good nutrition: it can heal or harm. Ultimately, health starts in your Forever Kitchen with fresh, unprocessed, nutritionally dense whole foods, a few herbs and spices, some tools and utensils, and an eagerness to boost your companion's health and longevity. One bite at a time.

The *Forever* Kitchen

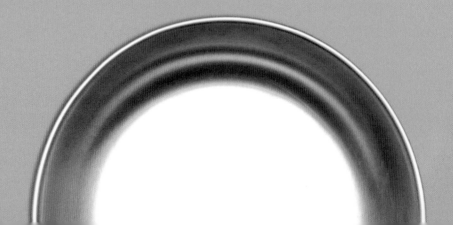

chapter 1

Feeding Your
FOREVER PET

What Does Your Forever Pet Need?

To decode the riddle of *exactly* what your pet needs to eat for a lifetime of good health, we should first look to the past.

Dogs have evolved alongside humans for millennia, which has influenced everything from their behavior to their gut microbiome. Siberian archaeological records indicate there were critical shifts in dog foraging and diets during the Holocene era, which began around twelve thousand years ago. This transition contributed to canines having much greater dietary diversity compared to their ancestor wolves. During the Holocene era, dogs started to scavenge, hunt small prey, eat marine and freshwater foods, and consume human leftovers. These feeding patterns and choices shaped their current nutrient requirements, demonstrating that dogs have a long-standing primal need for meat, fish, foraged fruits and vegetables, and the fresh foods that humans cook. These foods are key to a pet's longevity.

The Basics of Nutrition

What pets *don't* need are refined carbohydrates. Even though carbohydrates are a quick source of glucose (and glucose converts to energy), studies show that dogs and cats don't prefer them. In fact, when given a choice of what to eat, they pick carbs last.

Yet many bags of dry pet food contain up to 50 percent carbohydrates. This is bad news because carbs convert to starch, then sugar. Sugar feeds inflammation, and inflammation kick-starts a host of negative biologic processes. For example, puppies fed high-carb dry food have a significantly higher risk for atopy (doggy allergies) later in life. Thankfully, adding in as little as 20 percent fresh food dramatically reduces these chances.

While dogs and cats don't require added starch to be healthy, they do need healthy sources of fiber to maintain a thriving microbiome, and consumption of only protein and healthy fats are inadequate for this purpose.

Their gastrointestinal ecosystems need fiber-dense roughage (aka the prebiotic fibers that constitute "good carbs") without the added glycemic index/sugar spike of consuming refined, highly processed starch. The "good carbs/bad carbs" discussion can be summed up by most nutritionists in one statement: there's a big metabolic difference between eating broccoli and eating white bread. Paper after paper shows both dogs and cats require appropriate amounts of healthy fiber from fresh, minimally processed produce for healthy gut terrain, not to mention fruits and veggies are the most abundant source of vital naturally occurring antioxidants, phytonutrients, polyphenols, and bioactive plant compounds.

Refined carbs are out, and meat, fish, and fresh, whole foods are in. But how do you put that plan into action? The gist of it is simple: start swapping up, replacing poor-quality, "feed-grade" big-box store-bought treats and the unhealthy human food leftovers you give your pup with nutritious homemade options. Instead of pizza crusts, offer broccoli and mushroom stems. Rather than ultra-processed treats from a sealed bag, reach for sardines. Small swaps can equal big nutritional gains over time.

Veterinarians generally adhere to the "10 percent" rule, meaning that no more than 10 percent of daily calories should come from "extras," including longevity-boosting fresher foods in the form of treats, toppers, and mix-ins (nutrient-dense foods you add to whatever they're currently eating). Your healthy treat and meal topper options are limited only by your imagination, and we can't wait to see what #foreverbowl creations you come up with!

Once you've improved the quality and nutritional value of your treats and meal toppers (meaning all the "extras" have been cleaned up), you may decide to make your first nutritionally balanced homemade meal. Recipes for those start in chapter 4 on page 152. Treats differ from meals in that our complete and balanced recipes are formulated to *exceed* the recommended daily allowances for all required macronutrients, vitamins, and minerals. Treats in this book provide antioxidants, polyphenols, and phytonutrients, but they cannot be substituted for a complete and balanced diet. You're welcome to use the food recipes you make on lick mats, to fill interactive toys, as toppers on your pet's current diet, or to replace a little or all of what you are currently feeding. Just realize you'll need to reduce the amount of old food you're feeding as you increase the amount of fresh, homemade food, to account for the correct number of daily calories. Our advice has always been to feed as much fresh food as you can afford to feed and make changes at a pace that doesn't cause stress to you or your animals.

LEAST
ADULTERATED
FOODS

| HOMEMADE | RAW \| Pathogen Controlled | GENTLY COOKED | FREEZE-DRIED | DEHYDRATED |

Commercial Dog Food

Can you still feed your dog or cat commercial food? Of course! We are not advocating that you must make every one of your companion's meals by hand. When choosing healthy pet foods, try to keep the refined carbs to a minimum and aim for the bulk of calories to come from protein and fat (allowing for 10 percent wiggle room for healthy treats and toppers). If you do feed commercial pet food, rotate brands and proteins often, and aim to buy minimally processed (the least heat-adulterated) foods. The more processed a commercial pet food is, the more unwanted chemical by-products of high-heat processing will be present. Look for dehydrated, freeze-dried, gently cooked, or raw (generally found in the freezer section of your pet food retailer or online).

As you're evaluating the most high-quality food to buy, remember that the fewer bad carbs it contains, the better. In order to determine the amount in your pet's food, follow these simple guidelines:

1. Look for the Guarantee Analysis on your dry food label.
2. Do a little math:

Protein + Fat + Fiber + Moisture + Ash (if not listed, use 6 percent) = X

100–X = PERCENT CARBS

Aim to find a dog food with less than 20 percent carbs (and ideally 10 percent)

MOST
ADULTERATED FOODS

CANNED   **AIR-DRIED**   **BAKED**   **DRY** | Extruded   **SEMI-MOIST**

Processing terms can be tricky, so organizations such as the International Food Information Council have created classifications (including NOVA) that indicate the degree of processing. While the definitions can be subjective, this is what we mean:

- Minimally processed: Fresh or frozen pet food with no or only one thermal (heat) or pressure (high-pressure pasteurization) processing step.

- Processed: The previous category's (minimally processed) definition modified by an additional thermal (heat) process. This includes gently cooked dog food diets and freeze-dried or dehydrated diets made with ingredients that were previously processed (not raw).

- **Ultra-processed:** Fractioned, recombined foods with added ingredients, meaning dry, canned, or manufactured using several thermal or pressure processing steps for the final product.

Here's a handy way to distinguish the least processed foods from the most:

Minimally Processed	Processed	Ultra-Processed
corn	canned corn	corn chips
carrot	carrot juice	carrot cake
balanced homemade	commercially cooked	dry kibble

Stocking Your Forever Kitchen:
Tools, Dishes, and Utensils

A few essential tools and utensils will go a long way in making food preparation and serving easy. Stock up on these items and follow these tips as you build your Forever Kitchen.

Food Scale

A high-quality food scale can fit in the corner of your kitchen or in a drawer and should cost you around $20. In our complete and balanced recipes, we list measurements in ounces and grams because that's the standard for pet food cookbooks, so look for one that reads as such. You should also make sure it has a tare function, which means it will subtract the weight of the container you use for measuring.

Speaking of containers: your food scale should have a weighing surface large enough to hold a container or a removable bowl that can hold wet or dry food. You may be making several servings of food—and you may have a large dog with a big appetite—so always consider your serving size needs.

Cutting Board

There are as many kinds of cutting boards as there are dog breeds, but we like stone, natural hardwood (maple is the most popular and the most bacteria-resistant!), glass, or formaldehyde-free bamboo boards. Avoid plastic or melamine boards, as they contain microplastics (from 14–71 million polyethylene and 79 million polypropylene particles!) and chemicals (including formaldehyde) that may lead to cell changes and kidney damage. Steer clear of antibacterial boards, too. They may *sound* healthier, but they contain a chemical called triclosan, which has been linked to liver, thyroid, and inhalation toxicity.

Should you buy a different cutting board for your dog's food? Not necessarily. Just be sure to use one board exclusively for cutting raw meat because of the risk of bacterial contamination.

Food and Water Bowls

Dog bowls are one of the dirtiest places in your entire house, and the clear film that settles at the bottom is called biofilm, a slippery, slimy brew of bacteria that can be transferred from your dog to you. No matter which bowl you choose, make sure you're washing it after every meal. What type of bowl is best?

- **Plastic:** No! Plastic bowls grow the largest number of pathogens of any type of bowl. Plastics can also leach endocrine- and melanin-disrupting chemicals that cause contact dermatitis, a condition that leaves your animal's muzzle red and irritated. For more on plastics, see "Food Storage" on page 18.

- **Ceramic:** Be careful! Ceramic bowls harbor colonies of the most *harmful* bacteria, including *salmonella*, *E. Coli*, and *MRSA*. Ceramics can also contain lead, so if you opt for ceramic, make sure it's marked as being food-safe and lead-free, and disinfect it daily. Replace when you see fine lines and superficial cracks in the surface.

- **Stainless steel:** Yes, though cheaper brands have been involved in recalls due to heavy metal contamination. Be sure to buy high-quality bowls (eighteen-gauge metal) from a trusted source.

- **Kitchen-safe glass:** Yes. Durable, kitchen-friendly glass bowls, such as Pyrex®, make great food and water bowls for animals and don't pose a breaking risk.

- **What about lick mats and food holders?** Yes, but clean and replace regularly. While silicone and rubber lick mats and food holders/treat release toys are safe for the short time they are in use, they can retain food odors and stains.

Washing and Disinfecting Bowls: Wash your bowl after every meal. At least once a week, run your bowl through the hot cycle in your dishwasher or spray or coat it with hydrogen peroxide or white vinegar (do not mix the two), wait five minutes, then wipe with a clean sponge.

Water Filters

From 2010–2017, around one hundred thousand cases of cancer in the United States were linked to the chemicals (including arsenic, uranium, and radium) found in tap water. To prevent you *and* your animals from being harmed by chemicals in your water, first *test your water*. While you can call your local water company and ask for a water quality report for your area and a free test kit, these kits only cover the basic contaminants like lead (and not many others). The Environmental Working Group (EWG) has an extensive tap water database on their site (indicating everything that's been tested in your local water) so we encourage you to visit them at www.ewg.org/tapwater/.

After you know what's in your water, you can buy the right filter for it, including:

- **Carbon block filter:** You will have to replace yours more often, and they can be expensive, but they are the most effective at removing harmful chemicals. They do not, however, remove arsenic and perchlorate.

- **Granulated carbon filters:** Typically less effective than carbon filters, but less expensive.

- **Reverse osmosis filters:** These are terrific at removing contaminants like arsenic, fluoride, hexavalent chromium, nitrates, and perchlorate, but they don't remove endocrine disruptors or volatile organic compounds (VOCs), and they also remove helpful nutrients like iron, calcium, and magnesium.

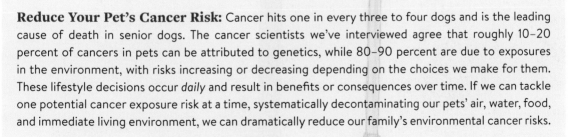

Reduce Your Pet's Cancer Risk: Cancer hits one in every three to four dogs and is the leading cause of death in senior dogs. The cancer scientists we've interviewed agree that roughly 10–20 percent of cancers in pets can be attributed to genetics, while 80–90 percent are due to exposures in the environment, with risks increasing or decreasing depending on the choices we make for them. These lifestyle decisions occur *daily* and result in benefits or consequences over time. If we can tackle one potential cancer exposure risk at a time, systematically decontaminating our pets' air, water, food, and immediate living environment, we can dramatically reduce our family's environmental cancer risks.

Food Storage

Whether you're storing toppers, treats, complete meals, powders, or supplements, glass is the way to go. It harbors fewer pathogens than other materials, doesn't contain dangerous ingredients, and doesn't leach those toxins into food. While we like heating foods the old-fashioned way, on the stovetop, if a microwave must be used, glass storage containers are a must.

Avoid plastic containers because:

- Plastics leach chemicals into your pet's food, including bisphenol A (BPA), which mimics hormones and can lead to cell changes that may cause cancer. Even BPA-free plastics aren't chemical-free. They're often made with bisphenol S (BPS), which can disrupt cellular functioning, affect the nervous system, and—even more than BPA—harm the reproductive system.

- Many plastics contain per- and polyfluoroalkyl substances (PFAS), fluorine-based substances that have been linked to certain cancers, low birth weight, immune disorders, and thyroid disease. These are also known as "forever chemicals" because they don't break down in our bodies or in the environment.

- Plastics contain phthalates, which disrupt the endocrine systems of not only our pets, but also wildlife, causing testicular impairment, genital deformations, low sperm counts, and infertility in species tested, including polar bears, deer, whales, and otters.

- Plastics are porous, meaning oils become trapped in them. Unless they're washed *daily*, which isn't practical, the food stored inside can be spoiled by rancid oils.

While rubber and silicone storage containers are certainly safer than plastic, they do absorb food smells over time and can be hard to clean. Again, choose glass.

Other Useful Kitchen Items

Kitchen shears	Use these for cutting herbs and meat.
Mini whisk	A smaller whisk may come in handy for recipes with smaller portions.
Silicone baking mats, parchment paper, and/or baking sheets	For easy, non-stick cooking.
Pizza cutter	A quick way to cut up batches of treats and jerkies.
Micro-grater	Can help you easily add a touch of ginger, turmeric, or a small amount of veggies to a bowl.
Food processor or blender	We love both for quickly mincing vegetables and herbs and pureeing some foods.
Slow cooker (Crock-Pot)	Great for gently cooking complete and balanced meals, making broths, or creating amazing home scents.
Ice cube trays	Terrific for making and storing training treats and toppers.
Mortar and pestle	Great for crushing up vitamin and mineral supplements, which are used in some of our complete and balanced recipes. You can also use an electric coffee grinder or small blender.
Dehydrator	Can convert everything that's about to expire in your refrigerator to shelf-stable on-the-go treats. Unlike ovens, you can run them all day without worrying—and they use less energy. At as little as $40, many are affordable, too.

Stocking Your Forever Kitchen:
Produce

When you're shopping for produce to stock in your Forever Kitchen, these are things you should look for and bear in mind.

Try to Choose Organic

Organic means that a product was grown or raised without the use of chemical fertilizers, pesticides, or other toxins. Not only are organic products free of many substances linked to health issues, but some organic produce is more nutritious, including being higher in polyphenols (powerful antiaging molecular compounds that reduce oxidative stress on tissues and organs) as well as bioactive compounds that fight cancer, promote heart health, boost brainpower, and prevent diabetes.

polyphenol level **CONVENTIONAL** FRUIT & VEGETABLES   **VS.**   *polyphenol level* **ORGANIC** FRUIT & VEGETABLES

Washing Organic Produce

Organic produce still carries the potential for bacterial contamination, so you *do* need to wash it, but you don't need to scrub or peel it for your pets. In fact, organic farming promotes a healthier, more diverse microbial environment in the soil, as opposed to conventional farming, so a little bit of healthy soil residue may actually be beneficial. Just be sure to dry your produce thoroughly after washing to prevent mold growth (we like using a salad spinner or spreading produce out on a paper towel).

How should you wash your produce? Here are two of our favorite ways:

Saltwater Produce Soak

While the FDA recommends you wash leafy vegetables with a diluted bleach solution, we prefer a saltwater soak. Washing cabbage for twenty minutes in a 10 percent saltwater solution (as opposed to vinegar or plain water) is more effective at removing common pesticides, including chlorpyrifos, DDT, cypermethrin, and chlorothalonil.

½ cup Himalayan or sea salt

5 cups filtered water

1. In a clean bowl, mix salt and filtered water together until the salt dissolves.

2. Soak fruits and vegetables in the solution for twenty minutes.

3. Rinse clean and dry thoroughly.

Vegetable Wax Remover

A vinegar soak is the most effective way to remove the wax coatings on produce, which are used to make apples, cucumbers, bell peppers, eggplants, and more look shiny.

½ cup filtered water

½ cup vinegar (white or apple cider)

1 tablespoon fresh lemon juice

2 tablespoons salt

1. In a clean bowl, mix ingredients.

2. Soak produce in the mixture. Delicate greens and berries should only soak for 2–3 minutes, while heartier produce like broccoli, cauliflower, and produce with thick peels can soak for 20–30 minutes.

3. Rinse clean and dry thoroughly.

Food Myths, Misconceptions, and Concerns

The amount of misinformation floating around about what's safe for your pet—and what isn't—is dizzying! We have some good news: your pet is safer than you probably think. Use caution and follow these tips.

Which Foods Are Considered Choking Hazards?

Almost all foods can be choking hazards to small kids and pets, depending on how they're served, and food items that are smaller than your dog's trachea pose a choking risk if accidently inhaled. Use common sense, and if you worry something is too big for your pet, chop it up or skip it. Follow these tips as well:

- Only feed the edible parts of fruits and veggies.
- Don't feed your kids (two- or four-legged) any tough stems or leaves of plants, pits, cores, or rinds.
- Choose treat sizes and molds that are twice the diameter of your dog's paw.
- Be careful with dogs that try to swallow everything whole.
- Chop all foods into bite-sized pieces.

Which Foods Are Toxic to Pets?

The European Pet Food Industry Federation (FEDIAF) says to avoid these foods entirely because they can cause illness—and even death.

- **Chocolate:** Contains theobromine, a chemical that acts as a diuretic, heart stimulant, blood vessel dilator, and a smooth muscle relaxant. Along with the caffeine in chocolate, dogs can't metabolize theobromine well.
- **Grapes (and raisins, sultanas, currants):** These contain a substance called tartaric acid, which may cause vomiting, thirst, diarrhea, and kidney damage.
- **Macadamia nuts:** Scientists don't know what toxin—if any—is poisonous to dogs, but their high fat content can lead to nausea.
- **Onions:** Onions contain thiosulfate, which can cause Heinz body anemia, a condition in which the red blood cells break down faster than the body can replace them. This leads to weakness and lethargy.

The following foods are not toxic for your pet:

- **Avocados:** The myth that avocados are toxic to pets is based on *one* study of two malnourished South African dogs who ate the *stems and leaves* of avocados. This study highlights why to keep your pet away from plant stems and leaves, not avocado flesh. (Your pet should also not eat stems and leaves from many plants, including tomato plants and walnut trees.) Avocado pits and skins are also a choking hazard, so don't feed these parts.

- **Peaches, cherries, apricots, and other pitted fruits:** These are perfectly safe, just remove the pits and stems.

- **Rosemary:** Rosemary does not cause seizures. But if your pet is epileptic, avoid feeding large quantities of rosemary *essential oil* or *extract* (which contains the concentrated compound camphor and can increase seizure risk in epileptic mammals).

- **English walnuts, almonds, pecans, and other nuts (except macadamia nuts):** No toxins identified. They can be a choking hazard, however, so chop them into small pieces. The outer casings of several nuts contain juglone, a compound that can cause a variety of symptoms, so always remove hulls and shells.

- **Pork:** There's a rumor that you shouldn't feed your pet pork because it has a high fat content. However, pork has around one-third the amount of fat of beef. Pork is an excellent source of protein and amino acids and can be a perfect protein for pets allergic to chicken or beef. If serving raw, the Centers for Disease Control (CDC) recommend you should freeze pork for twenty days at 5°F (-15°C) to kill any *trichinella*. Cooking to 145°F also inactivates any potential parasites.

- **Salmon:** Consuming raw salmon sourced from the Pacific Northwest can (rarely) cause a parasitic condition in dogs called "salmon poisoning." The good news is freezing (-20°C for twenty-four hours) or gently cooking removes this small risk.

- **Garlic:** Since it's part of the onion family, people often assume it's unsafe. But garlic contains only one-fifteenth the amount of thiosulfate as onions and has been declared safe for pets in a national report. It also contains allicin, a medicinal compound that can help your dog's cardiovascular system, which is why you see garlic added to lots of commercial dry pet foods.

- **Mushrooms:** All mushrooms that promote health in humans also do so for pets, and we love feeding mushrooms for their medicinal compounds. Cooking mushrooms makes them easier to digest and enhances their health benefits (for instance, it inactivates agaritine—a mycotoxin, or toxic mold, found in portobello mushrooms)

I've Heard You Should Never Feed Your Pet Fresh Food. Is That True?

No, and here's why.

Many veterinary schools and teaching hospitals have affiliations with large pet food companies that manufacture ultra-processed foods. Because these companies don't currently sell fresh food diets, students are not taught about pet foods besides dry and canned products. In fact, many vet students graduate indoctrinated with the notion that pets should *only* be fed highly refined, ultra-processed diets throughout life and that feeding *any* other type of food could be dangerous.

The problem is: emerging science doesn't back up this opinion, nor does common sense. The entire animal kingdom needs a variety of fresh foods for optimal health. And most pets never get *any*.

Just look at the long-lived canines we described in the introduction. Most of these animals never ate highly processed pet food, and that did nothing to diminish their Forever Dog status.

Now to the other dirty little secret about why fresh food and treats are superior. In the United States, all food is inspected. Food that passes inspection is deemed approved for human consumption. Food that fails inspection is deemed "feed grade," meaning it's turned into animal feed, including pet food. "Feed grade" ingredients, by definition, have more contaminants of every kind.

Garlic Guidelines: If you want to add some fresh garlic to your pet's meal routine, here are some suggested daily amounts:

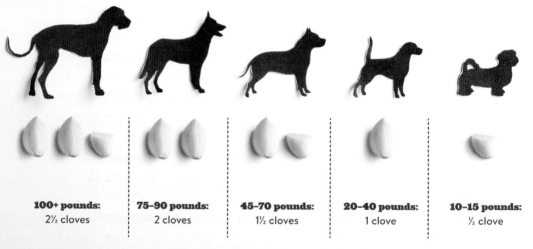

100+ pounds:	75–90 pounds:	45–70 pounds:	20–40 pounds:	10–15 pounds:
2½ cloves	2 cloves	1½ cloves	1 clove	½ clove

The National Research Council has set a historical safe intake for cats to be 17 mg/kg of body weight.

Can I Change My Animal's Food?

Absolutely. If you want to work toward having a Forever Pet, incorporating a variety of nutrient-dense, fresher foods is a must.

If your companion has been eating the same brand and flavor of food for a while, their microbiome (and in turn, their immune system) will benefit from some nutritional diversity. Your goal is to reduce your pet's metabolic stress and inflammation, clear out toxins, activate longevity pathways, and re-balance the microbiome. Feeding a variety of whole, healthy meals and snacks will ensure you can do that.

The pace and frequency of new food introductions, however, is based on several factors, including your animal's ability to adapt to new foods and the food storage space in your kitchen. In order to swap up in the best possible manner, offer new foods slowly, one bite at a time, using the quality of your pet's stool as a barometer of when to introduce more new foods. If your animal's poop loosens, don't introduce more new foods or continue to increase the amount of new food or treats. Allow the gut time to adjust to changes, and when the stool firms up again, proceed with more food diversification. We'll dive more into transitioning to a new food on page 160.

Can I Feed My Pet Table Scraps?

If diets primarily consisting of healthy leftovers have sustained millions of dogs throughout history, chances are human food treats and meals will work for your pet, too.

However, there is a difference between leftover steamed broccoli and leftover French fries. Unwholesome leftovers result in unhealthy bodies, and wholesome leftovers result in a more diversified microbiome and improved overall health. In fact, feeding healthy human leftovers and making at least 20 percent of a puppy's food intake a raw meat diet may contribute to puppies having a much lower incidence of atopy (allergies) later in life. Puppies who consume a nonprocessed (raw) meat-based diet have also been found to have a significantly lower risk of inflammatory bowel disease (IBD) later in life, compared to kibble-fed puppies.

Choose healthfully prepared meats, fruits, and veggies to share with your animals, without sauces, sugar, or spicy condiments added. Don't share fried, charred, or spoiled food. Stick to sharing the "good carbs" (low-glycemic, high-fiber veggies), and bypass the refined carbs (breads, pasta, etc.). To prevent unwanted begging, we also recommend not sharing food while at the table; instead, give healthy human foods when training, or add them into your animal's bowl.

Pets Need Enrichment: Interactive toys (or, as we sometimes call them, "tasty activities") are designed to stimulate and engage, both physically and mentally. Puzzle toys, lick mats, stuffable chew toys, and DIY food games and snacks provide healthy distraction (when needed), entertainment, boredom relief, sensory stimulation, and enrichment. You can customize the activity, toy, and treat to your animal's personality, needs, and dietary goals, and you can upcycle your family's healthy leftovers for your animals, in the following ways:

- Spoon into ice cube trays and freeze to use as meal toppers.

- Load in an interactive/treat release toy and feed or freeze.

- Smear on lick mats and freeze for a tasty distraction later on.

- Mix a few tablespoons of leftovers with a little stock or broth and make pupsicles or other frozen treats.

Are Fats Good or Bad for My Pet?

Many pet parents fear fat for a variety of reasons, and some fears are justified. Reheated, oxidized, and rancid fats (the recycled grease sprayed on many dry foods as a "palatant") are horrible pet food additives, flooding the body with advanced lipoxidation end products (ALEs). ALEs are some of the most cellularly damaging tagalongs of industrially produced pet food, contributing to pancreatitis, nausea, GI issues, and early aging.

However, unrefined, unadulterated raw fats are healthy fuel for the body, providing sustained energy exactly as nature intended. These fats, including DHA and EPA, are the building blocks for healthy cell membranes and cognitive well-being.

It's important to note that dogs and cats require different types of essential fatty acids to be added directly to their food, or they risk deficiencies. For instance, cats need to eat arachidonic acid (AA), an omega-6 fatty acid. Pets also can't convert plant sources of

alpha-linolenic acid (ALA) efficiently enough to DHA or EPA to meet their requirements, so they need to get it from foods like sardines. Finally, pets must be given the omega-6 fatty acid linoleic acid (LA), which is why you'll see the addition of certain plant oils in our complete and balanced recipes.

There are other types of healthy fats that provide health benefits but *don't* meet your animal's EPA or DHA requirements (that's okay, they're still terrific). We include some of these in our recipes:

- **Coconut oil:** Solid at room temperature, coconut oil is nature's richest source of lauric acid, a medium-chain fatty acid that helps fight yeast and raise HDL (good) cholesterol levels.

- **Black seed oil:** Also called black cumin seed oil (but unrelated to the cumin in your spice drawer), it has an impressive array of health benefits thanks to its thymoquinone, a phytochemical with powerful antioxidant qualities that can help alleviate neurodegenerative diseases, reduce cognitive decline and brain disorders, reduce pain and inflammation, and fight viruses and cancer.

- **Olive oil:** This heart-healthy monounsaturated fat contains oleic acid, which reduces inflammation.

Finally, while fat provides twice the calories of carbs or protein, fat is not the main reason so many pets are overweight. The consumption of excessive starch (which the body stores as fat) is the root cause of the obesity epidemic in companion animals. Dogs and cats need healthy fats—not starchy, refined carbs—for longevity fuel.

Can "Anti-Nutrients" Harm My Pet?

We can all agree that a plant-rich diet is good, but plants *do* produce some compounds (including lectins, glucosinolates, oxalates, phytates, saponins, and tannins) that may make other nutrients less bioavailable. These compounds—called "anti-nutrients"—are intended to protect plants from insects and diseases. But if you're feeding them to your pet in the hope they'll get nutrition from them, are you instead doing the opposite?

Probably not. Most nutritionists agree that the benefits of eating plants containing anti-nutrients outweigh the risks of not eating plants at all. Plants are where the bulk of our life-extending polyphenols, medicinal phytochemicals, antioxidants, and flavonoids come from. (Plus—let's be honest—every food ingredient, in isolation, has something "wrong" with it.) However, if these plant compounds are consumed in large amounts, for example, in vegan or some "grain-free" pet foods with a very high starch/carb content (see page 14 to calculate the amount of carbs in your pet food), the chances of having anti-nutrient issues from excessive plant material in the diet increases. For these reasons (among others), we do not recommend feeding your pet high-starch/carb or vegan pet foods.

Genetic or breed predispositions can also impair the body's ability to efficiently eliminate these compounds. If your animal has a specific health condition where your vet has suggested avoiding certain foods for certain reasons, there are plenty of alternatives you can choose from in this book. Finally—in case you're still worried about anti-nutrients—know that the overall plant material in our recipes is low, and that's because it reflects pets' ancestral intake. You can also cook your pet's food or try sprouting (see page 66), both of which inactivate or dramatically reduce many of these anti-nutrients.

Your Pet's Microbiome

Inside your companion's digestive system lives a complex and magnificent world, teeming with a life of its own. Made up of bacteria, viruses, fungi, parasites, and other microscopic friends and foes, the microbiome is central to your animal's health. It helps them digest food, metabolizes nutrients, is integrally involved in immune defenses, detoxifies contaminants and pathogens, regulates inflammatory pathways, produces and releases enzymes, balances the hormonal system, produces key vitamins, including B12 and K, and supplies chemicals that make essential brain and neurological functions possible. Your pet's gut health is also intimately linked to chronic diseases that can shorten their life span.

Unhealthy exposures that can throw off the diverse, well-balanced colonies of microbes inside your pet include household and environmental chemicals, fertilizers, antibiotics and other medications, stress, disease, and a monotonous, metabolically stressful diet. Research shows that a raw diet—as opposed to one composed of mostly heat-processed foods—promotes a more balanced and diverse community of gut bacteria *and* healthier gut functions, in addition to better digestion and fewer allergies later in life. Additionally, dogs who are regularly fed nonprocessed meats, organs, fish, eggs, raw bones, vegetables, and berries, are 22 percent less likely to develop issues such as chronic enteropathy (CE) as opposed to dogs who eat processed pet food.

In case you're still skeptical about the miraculous microbiome, let's look at Bobi. We submitted Bobi's poop for microbiome analysis, and one of the researchers said that Bobi has the most diverse and robust collection of microorganisms they have ever seen! Remember: Bobi never ate anything but freshly prepared foods, and he had extensive daily exposure to microbe-rich soil. Microbial ecologist Dr. Holly Ganz, who has spent her career examining how food impacts dogs' and cats' microbiomes, has also told us how shocking it is to look at poop under a microscope and notice which pets have access to fresh foods, and which pets don't. Their microbiomes are vastly different, with the fresh food feces far more microbially diverse.

The microbiome is an area that we're pas-

Boost Your Bacteria: One of the most prevalent and important members of your animal's microbiome is the *Fusobacterium* species, whose bacteria are bolstered by feeding fresh, meat-based diets like the recipes in this book. While antibiotics are often necessary, even one round (including the antidiarrhea medicine metronidazole) obliterates the good gut guys, including *Fusobacteria*. Even when medications are discontinued, your animal's gut may never bounce back to normal. But don't panic; dogs fed a home-cooked diet had improved levels of *Fusobacteria* in the gut.

sionate about, so the recipes in this book contain specific ingredients that promote gut health. We chose our five Forever Food categories—mushrooms, sprouts and herbs, dandelions, eggs, and sardines and clean fish—in part because they contain beneficial nutrients, compounds, and prebiotic fibers that are all key players in cultivating a flourishing, healthy microbiome.

Prebiotic Fiber

Prebiotics are plant fibers that feed gut bacteria. Yes, the microbes in your animal's gut are living beings that require food to survive. Consuming prebiotic-rich foods is vital to a healthy gut, and www.foreverdog.com has a downloadable PDF that lists all the prebiotic-rich fresh fruits and veggies that make great training treats and rewards.

Pets with sensitive GI tracts who are fed diets higher in fiber have less gut inflammation; firmer, less runny poops; and saccharolysis (the breakdown of sugar into energy). These are all signs of a well-functioning microbiome.

Bolster Your Broccoli: We love sliced broccoli as a grab-and-go treat because broccoli helps prevent cancer and type 2 diabetes, and protects the lining of the small intestine. Allowing chopped broccoli to sit for ninety minutes before feeding it also increases the activity of sulforaphane—a phytochemical that may prevent and slow the growth of cancerous tumors—by as much as 2.8 times!

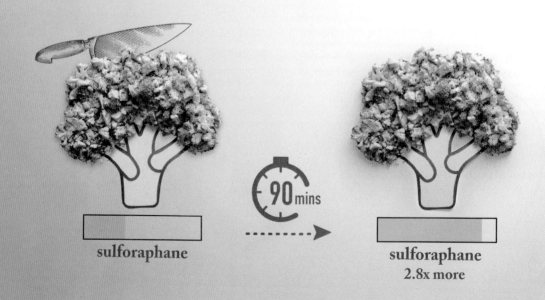

sulforaphane

90 mins

sulforaphane
2.8x more

Transitioning to Healthier Habits

Transitioning to a new way of feeding and treating your companion is all about instituting healthy habits. As a first step, we recommend revamping snacks (aka training treats, lures, or rewards). Treats will no longer be unhealthy, high-carb, processed junk food. Instead, healthy treats are used as intentional rewards, fed for a dual purpose: saying "good job" *and* creating health. Starting in chapter 3 on page 74, we'll provide many recipes for healthy treats, in addition to the following page's grab-and-go treat options that come directly from Mother Nature. We put interactive food toys and food brain games in the "treat" category, too, because the foods used to engage in these boredom-busting enrichment activities aren't always nutritionally complete and balanced meals.

Once you've updated your pet's snacking habits, you can move along to revamping your animal's meals. Remember, you don't have to transition to *all* homemade meals; you can swap up and replace whatever your animal is currently eating with 10–75 percent home-made food. Complete and balanced home-made meals are chock-full of fresh, whole foods, and soon, you may notice health, food preferences, and energy levels change as their bodies repair and improve themselves from the inside out.

Just remember that swapping up isn't an all-or-nothing approach. In fact, it's an *everything* approach. The only rule to mixing and matching all types of pet foods, in any/ all amounts, is to blend at a pace that doesn't cause any gastrointestinal (GI) upset for your animals. It's perfectly safe to feed a mash-up of homemade and commercially prepared diets, and raw and cooked foods, just as we can eat a variety of cooked and raw foods in the same meal without causing bodily harm. There's not one single research paper demonstrating any negative repercussions for pets eating a variety of foods, so feel free to add raw toppers to commercial pet foods, cooked toppers (or your leftover cooked veggies) on raw meals, or lick mats and interactive toys smeared and stuffed with every possible combination you can think of.

How to Freeze Meat: If you have concerns about potential parasites in fresh meats from your grocery store, an easy thing to remember is "Freeze for 3": place all butcher shop purchases in the freezer for three weeks prior to thawing and preparing for your family (two- or four-legged).

Grab-and-Go Treats: Fresh Pharma from the Fridge You Can Share Right Now

Also known as Core Longevity Toppers (or CLTs), these are bits of raw or gently cooked fresh food you sprinkle on as toppers or chop up and feed as raw food treats. Instead of whipping up something from scratch, these CLTs may include leftovers, discarded bits and pieces of whole foods, or extra healthy tidbits you have lying around right now. Though they may seem small, they confer big benefits. For example, a study of Scottish terriers showed that adding bits of yellow, orange, and green leafy vegetables just three times a week to their bowls was associated with a *significant decrease* (more than 60 percent!) in the likelihood of developing bladder cancer.

Remember, all treats and "extras" should comprise less than 10 percent of daily calories.

Antioxidant-Rich

- Vitamin C–filled **bell peppers**
- Capsanthin-filled **red bell peppers**
- Anthocyanin-rich **blueberries, blackberries,** and **raspberries**
- Beta-carotene-rich **cantaloupe**
- Naringenin-filled **cherry tomatoes**
- Punicalagin-loaded **pomegranate seeds**
- Polyacetylene-loaded **carrots**
- Apigenin-loaded **peas**
- Sulforaphane-rich **broccoli**

Anti-Inflammatory

- Bromelain-filled **pineapple**
- Omega-3-dense **sardines** (except for dogs requiring a low-purine diet)
- Quercetin-rich **cranberries**
- Cucurbitacin-rich **cucumbers**
- Manganese-rich **coconut meat** (or dried, unsweetened coconut chips)
- Vitamin E–rich raw **sunflower seeds** (sprout them and other microgreens for a chlorophyll-rich upgrade from grass!)
- Magnesium-filled raw **pumpkin seeds** (feed seeds one at a time for perfect-sized training treats, up to ¼ teaspoon for every ten pounds of body weight, spread throughout the day)
- Selenium-rich **Brazil nuts** (chop up one a day for you and your big dog or share one with smaller dogs)
- Folate-filled **green beans**
- Fisetin-filled **strawberries**
- Indole-3-carbinol-rich **kale** (or homemade kale chips)
- Isothiocyanate-loaded **cauliflower**

Detox Delights

- Apigenin-loaded **celery**
- Anethole-filled **fennel**
- Fucoidan-rich **nori** (and other seaweeds)
- Betaine-filled **beetroot** (except for dogs with oxalate issues)

For Guts and Glory

- Prebiotic-rich **jicama**, **green bananas**, **sunchokes**, **asparagus**, **pumpkin**
- Actinidin-rich **kiwi**
- Pectin-rich **apples**
- Papain-rich **papaya**

Consider Cooking: While these grab-and-go vegetables are nutrient-dense raw, in some ways, they are better when cooked:

- **Spinach:** When spinach is exposed to heat, it releases its calcium, making it easier for the body to absorb it. It also reduces the oxalate load.

- **Asparagus:** Heat breaks down asparagus's tough cell walls, making it easier for the body to absorb its vitamins B9, C, and E.

- **Mushrooms:** Cooking releases the antioxidant ergothioneine, which helps protect against free radical damage. Baking mushrooms for 10 minutes at 200°F has also been shown to preserve the most flavonoids while improving digestibility.

- **Tomatoes:** Cooking increases the amount of bioavailable lycopene by 50 percent, which can help prevent heart disease and cancer. But it's a trade-off, as cooking *reduces* tomatoes' vitamin C content by 29 percent.

- **Carrots:** Carrots are rich in beta-carotene, which metabolizes into vitamin A and supports the immune system. Cooking increases their amount of beta-carotene.

- **Bell peppers:** Like tomatoes, heat breaks down the plant's cell walls and makes absorption of certain antioxidants easier. However—like tomatoes—it also reduces the vitamin C content.

- **Green beans:** Cooking increases their antioxidant levels.

- **Broccoli, cauliflower, and Brussels sprouts:** Cooking activates an enzyme called myrosinase, which then turns on the vegetables' cancer-fighting phytochemicals.

Transition Tips for Finicky Eaters

Some pets take to new foods right away, while others take more time. We've found the following strategies can help finicky eaters discover a new way of eating.

- **Be Consistent:** Begin by choosing a similar protein and food/treat consistency: If you currently feed beef-flavored canned food and beef soft treats, make poached beef recipes (stews) to start.

- **Aromas Help:** Heat homemade food, at least initially, to release an enticing aroma that can lure pets to their bowls. Once they're eating their new diet, you can decide to moderate recipe cooking times.

- **Sneak in New Treats:** Break current treats into pea-sized pieces and begin rotating in a new treat morsel every third or fourth bite. Increase new treats until you use up the old ones, and don't repurchase your former treats unless they're as high-quality as what you can make at home.

- **Don't Let Them Graze:** If you currently replenish the food bowl throughout the day (the all-you-can-eat buffet), pick up the bowl when they're finished.

- **Create an Eating Window:** See "Timing Matters" on page 36 for the benefits of creating an eating window.

- **Count Calories:** Identify the number of calories your pet needs on page 158, measure out those calories, in terms of the volume of food you are feeding, or food you want to feed, and stick to that amount. Overfeeding (keeping them full all the time) doesn't motivate your companion to try new foods.

- **Switch One Thing:** Changing the time that you feed, the amount that you feed, and what you feed all at once is too stressful. Modify one variable at a time, so you can track your animal's response.

- **Keep Trying:** Try previously snubbed foods over and over, throughout your animal's life. It took Karen's dog, Homer, three years to eat cucumbers. Just as our palates change and we learn to love or crave food we didn't like as kids, animals are open to eating a varied diet, depending on what they need—and when.

Just remember: Slow down if you see any type of physiologic stress (like loose poop) or behavioral stress (like refusal to eat by nightfall). And don't *you* stress. You have plenty of time to make slow but consistent changes that result in big health gains over time, so go at a pace that resonates with your animal's body and brain.

Remedies for GI Distress

If transitioning to healthier eating habits causes GI distress, first slow down. You can also try these natural, science-backed remedies.

- **Slippery Elm Powder:** Made from the inner bark of the slippery elm, a tree native to North America, slippery elm has been used by Indigenous people for centuries to relieve diarrhea and GI distress. Research backs this up, showing it's effective at relieving inflammatory bowel disease in humans. Slippery elm contains mucilage, a substance that turns into jelly when it's mixed with water and then coats and soothes whatever it touches. Our recommended dosage is ½ teaspoon for every ten pounds of body weight, mixed with bland food, twice daily.

- **Marshmallow Root Powder:** Made from the roots of a perennial flowering herb, this powder decreases inflammation, improves stool consistency, and prevents stomach ulcers. Try ¼ teaspoon for every fifteen pounds of body weight, mixed with bland food, twice daily.

- **Pumpkin:** Try a dollop of canned or steamed 100 percent pure pumpkin puree (one teaspoon per ten pounds of body weight). Pumpkin is rich in prebiotic fiber, which will help GI upset and loose stools.

- **Activated Charcoal:** Feed one capsule for every twenty-five pounds of weight.

The Poop Test: Your dog's poop is a surefire way to see how well they're transitioning to a new food.

- Your animal's gut is doing great! It's time to increase the amount of new, fresh food by 5–10 percent each day.

- Slow down and don't add in more new food until the poop firms up.

- Your dog is experiencing significant digestive upset with their new food. Add some pumpkin into their diet to firm up the poops, then proceed slowly.

Timing Matters

When your dog eats is just as important as what they eat. Your dog's microbiome, hormones, digestive system, and brain chemicals follow their circadian rhythm, so pay attention to when your dog is awake and ready to chow down. Mice who eat within an eight- to twelve-hour window have been shown to live longer than mice who eat all day—even though they consume the same amount of calories—so we advocate for targeted calorie consumption within a set period of time.

By creating an "eating window" of six to eight hours for dogs and eight to twelve hours for cats, you will maximize autophagy, your animal's cellular housecleaning and detoxification cycles during the nonfeeding times. Aim to stop all feeding two hours before bed, which allows the body time to switch from digestion mode to cell repair mode. You can feed your pet one, two, or three times a day; just do whatever is best for the family.

If your perfectly healthy dog doesn't appear to be hungry, let them skip a meal. Feed your animals when they show a desire to eat, and be sure to give them the same amount of calories they require a day (so you may be feeding fewer but bigger meals). There is no biological reason a dog can't fast for a bit; after all, Bobi and Darcy occasionally skipped meals, and, clearly, this did nothing to affect their Forever Dog status. A landmark study of almost twenty-five thousand dogs also revealed that those fed once a day are less likely to suffer from age-related conditions such as cancer, cognitive impairment, dental issues, and kidney or urinary issues.

chapter

2

FOREVER *Foods*

This chapter introduces our favorite Forever Foods, picked because they are packed with some of the most highly bioavailable nutritional benefits available. You can mix these foods into homemade meals, add as toppers, or feed as grab-and-go treats.

Forever Food:
Medicinal Mushrooms

Medicinal mushrooms are powerful yet misunderstood. They contain gut-nourishing prebiotic fibers, longevity-promoting ingredients (including polyphenols, glutathione, polyamines, and ergothioneine), and immune-boosting beta-glucans, making them a miracle-working Forever Food that's perfect for your pet.

Serving Suggestion: Add one teaspoon of cooked mushrooms
per ten pounds of body weight daily.

Mushrooms have been used as medicine for thousands of years—from the Ancient Greeks to the Roman Empire to the first century AD Moche people of Peru. Two thousand years ago, Chinese experts even called them "divine herbs that energize chi (Qi)" (or life force). Yet sometime in the Middle Ages, they got a bad rap, probably because—as we all now know—not all species are edible. Some wild mushrooms will kill you (and your pets) if consumed.

We think that something that's powerful enough to both cure and kill demands some respect.

The reality is if a mushroom is safe and healthy for humans, it's safe and healthy for other animals, including pets. If it's poisonous to humans, it's also poisonous to pets. When we talk about mushrooms, we mean edible, highly nutritious "medicinal" or "functional" mushrooms, a distinct group of safe fungi known for their exceptional health benefits beyond their nutrient composition. In addition to being nutritious culinary staples, medicinal mushrooms contain potent compounds that provide specific health benefits and may be turned into supplements regulated by the Food and Drug Administration (FDA).

Medicinal mushrooms that help our bodies be more resistant to physical, chemical, and biologic stress are called adaptogenic mushrooms. Thankfully, many of the culinary mushrooms found at the local grocery store or farmers' market contain some of our favorite adaptogenic compounds, and they are super versatile in how they can be incorporated into your animal's life, including teas, broths, toppers, lick mat schmears/toy stuffers, ice cubes, foods, and treats . . . Anything is possible with mushrooms!

Science proves again and again that mushrooms are detoxifying, cell-protecting, immune-modulating, brain-building, nutritious powerhouses that can benefit the whole body. In one study, individuals who ate mushrooms daily had a lower risk of premature death from all causes, *no matter what their diets or lifestyles were.* Mushrooms contain polyamines, compounds that increase autophagy, which is the cell's ability to shed and recycle its old parts. One of those polyamines is spermidine, which improves cognition and protects the nervous system. *Mushrooms contain more spermidine than any other food.* They're also chock-full of glutathione—a powerful internal antioxidant that protects the cells, but that animals produce less of as they age—and ergothioneine (ERGO), another antioxidant that increases anti-inflammatory hormones and decreases oxidative stress. Both glutathione and ERGO are nicknamed "longevity vitamins" in the science world today.

Medicinal mushrooms can also fight viruses and harmful bacteria, balance blood sugar, help prevent inflammation, and promote a healthy gut microbiome. Mushrooms can lower the risk of cancer by up to 45 percent (if you eat only two a day!), reduce the risk of depression and anxiety, and fight chronic inflammation (especially in the brain). This is key, since chronic inflammation leads to cognitive decay, cardiovascular issues, and organ failure—central factors in a shorter, less healthy life.

Make the mighty mushroom a central part of your pet's Forever Food intake!

Mushroom Feeding 101: Some medicinal mushrooms are becoming so popular in certain markets that they're marketed as "super healthy gourmet mushrooms," including shiitake, turkey tail, maitake, reishi, shimeji, oyster, cordyceps, and lion's mane. In your pet's meals, you can also use some of the more common mushrooms found at your local grocery store or farmers' market, like portobello, white, or button mushrooms. Most mushrooms can be eaten fresh, dried, powdered, or as supplements, but we love to sauté them in raw butter or coconut oil for a quick topper or make them into a hearty broth or tea. Freeze mushroom broth for a tasty, hydrating treat, or use it in homemade meal recipes.

If you can't find fresh culinary mushrooms, look for dried mushrooms or whole-food mushroom powders in Asian markets, farmers' markets, and supplement or herb retailers. Dried mushrooms can be rehydrated in bone broth or herbal tea prior to being added to recipes. Don't let your dog forage wild mushrooms in the backyard, and if they *do* ingest wild mushrooms, take them to the emergency room immediately.

Try one variety at a time, or mix and match as a daily treat or topper, following the dosage instruction on page 39.

Medicinal Mushrooms: Their Adaptogenic Properties and Cooking Notes

These images illustrate the "ideal" medicinal mushrooms, but some may be hard to source, so feel free to use common culinary mushrooms like portobello, white button, porcini, and cremini.

Type	Benefits	In the Kitchen
Reishi 	• Lowers cortisol • Contains over 140 triterpenes (particularly ganoderic acids, lucidenic acids, and sterols), which are highly anti-inflammatory, antimicrobial, and antiviral chemical compounds that regulate the immune system and fight cancer cells • Balances blood sugar • Loaded with beta-glucans that stimulate innate immune responses against cancer cells • Supports liver detoxification	Small mushrooms are great for sautéing, but large ones can be quite hard, so boil in water to make a broth or tea.
Chaga 	• Prevents liver inflammation • Suppresses cancer growth (up to 60 percent tumor suppression in mice) • Full of antioxidants, including triterpenoids, melanins, polysaccharides, polyphenols, and flavans • Immune balancing (often used with allergic conditions)	Typically available as a supplement or powder. Fresh chaga is too hard to eat, so boil to make broth or tea.
Lion's Mane (also called Yamabushitake) 	• Improves cognitive impairment • Helps grow neurons • Stimulates nerve growth factor (NGF) for nerve support and repair • Regulates mood • Improves the gut microbiome of aging dogs • Contains antiaging polysaccharides and peptides	Can be cooked, boiled, or eaten raw. They taste a bit like seafood.

Type	Benefits	In the Kitchen
Turkey Tail 	• Slows the growth of Hemangiosarcoma, a highly malignant cancer • Contains prebiotic fibers to improve the microbiome • Inhibits the production of certain cytokines, which reduces inflammation	Great for boiling to make tea/broth, ice cubes, or drying
Maitake (also called **Hen of the Woods**) 	• Contains d-fraction, a potent anti-tumor and immune-boosting polysaccharide • Contains beta-glucans that help heal the gut • Contains alpha-glucans that positively influence glucose and insulin metabolism	Great for boiling or sautéing
Oyster 	• Pleuran, one of the bioactives in oyster mushrooms, benefits lung health. • Phenolics decrease blood pressure. • Can inhibit the growth of breast and colon cancer cells • Immune-boosting	These grow soft and delicate when they're sautéed.
Shiitake 	• Contains the bioactive substance lentinan, which enhances immune function and slows the growth of tumors • Antiviral • Contains L-ergothioneine, whose antioxidant properties fight free radicals	They are terrific for sautéing and are frequently found dried.

Type	Benefits	In the Kitchen
Cremini or White (**also called Button**) 	• High in protein • Contains polysaccharides that improve insulin resistance and act as probiotics to improve gut health	Easy to sauté, grill, or dehydrate
Portobello 	• Contains more potassium than bananas • Helps prevent neurodegenerative diseases	Easy to sauté, grill, or dehydrate
Cinnamon Cap 	• Contains polysaccharides that reduce inflammation • Contains beta-glucans that act on cell receptors to reduce cholesterol	Grows on stumps and roots. Great for sautéing.
Shimofuri Hiratake (**also called Black Pearl**) 	• Inhibits the development of breast and colon cancer cells • Contains lovastatin, a statin that reduces cholesterol	Great in soups or stews. Good for sautéing.

Type	Benefits	In the Kitchen

Shimeji
(also called White Beech or
Seafood Mushroom)

- Antimicrobial and antiparasitic
- Anticancer
- Protects the heart

They are bitter until
you cook them.

Cordyceps

- Increases energy (ATP) production
- Supports gut, heart, and kidney
  health by improving metabolic
  pathways
- Changes gene expression, which
  bestows antiaging benefits
- Contains chemical compounds
  (including cyclodepsipeptides,
  nucleosides, and polysaccharides)
  with immune-regulating,
  antioxidant, antitumor, anticancer,
  anti-inflammatory, anti-allergic,
  antibacterial, and antifungal
  properties

Typically found in a
powder form or in a
supplement. If fresh,
you can boil them.

Chaga, the Weird Mushroom: Chaga doesn't look like a mushroom at all. This weird parasitic fungus grows on trees and resembles charcoal or bark. Known for its anticancer and liver-healing benefits (it even decreases tumor growth in dogs with bladder cancer), you can buy chaga chunks, tincture, or powder and use it to make tea, or throw a chunk in your bone broth pot.

A Mushroom Is a Mushroom Is a Mushroom: Button (or white) mushrooms are the same thing as cremini mushrooms (one is white, and one is brown). And creminis are the same variety as portobellos. That's right, they are all *Agaricus bisporus*, and they are simply at different stages of maturing. As buttons and creminis grow into portobellos, they lose water, which makes the bigger variety more flavorful.

Mushroom Hacks

To boost the nutritional benefits of your mushrooms and save time and money, follow these tips:

- **Increase Vitamin D Levels:** Mushrooms are loaded with vitamin D2 (ergocalciferol), a form of vitamin D that is as biologically active as vitamin D3 (cholecalciferol) in dogs (but not cats). In order to boost vitamin D levels, wash mushrooms, then place them directly in the sun, upside down, with their gills exposed, for at least fifteen minutes. This will boost your button mushroom's vitamin D by up to 15 percent, and a shiitake mushroom can increase its vitamin D content by 1,150 times after eight hours.

- **Don't Throw Out the Stems:** They have two times the bioactive fiber (which helps your dog's digestion) and beta-glucans (which balance the immune system, help regulate insulin, reduce inflammation, and support the gastrointestinal system) as the caps. Ask a vendor at your local farmers' market if they have stems for sale. Often they cut them off and will sell them to you for cheap.

- **Cook Your Mushrooms:** All the mushroom experts we've interviewed say that cooking mushrooms prior to feeding them is the best way to deliver the most bioactive compounds, including polyphenols and antioxidants, which *increase* with cooking. The healthiest way to cook mushrooms is to poach them: chop to desired size and add to a pan with enough broth, tea, or filtered water to allow them to simmer in liquid. Cook until tender. Finicky animals will prefer mushrooms sautéed in coconut oil or a dab of raw butter.

- **Slice Faster:** Use an egg slicer. This is especially helpful with button mushrooms.

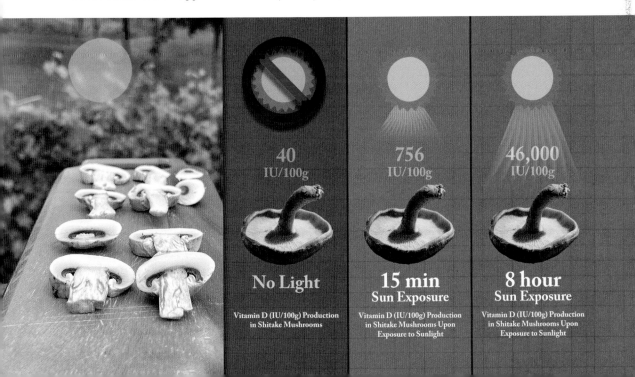

40 IU/100g	756 IU/100g	46,000 IU/100g
No Light	**15 min** Sun Exposure	**8 hour** Sun Exposure
Vitamin D (IU/100g) Production in Shitake Mushrooms	Vitamin D (IU/100g) Production in Shitake Mushrooms Upon Exposure to Sunlight	Vitamin D (IU/100g) Production in Shitake Mushrooms Upon Exposure to Sunlight

Forever Food:
Eggs

Eggs are the most nutritious dog snack on earth. A powerful protein that contains virtually all the essential amino acids, vitamins, and minerals your pet needs, eggs also provide vital antioxidants and double the amount of choline (per one hundred grams) as any other food. Eggs are nature's multivitamin!

Serving Suggestion: Feed ½ egg per ten pounds of body weight three times per week.

Sometime, around the dawn of time, primitive people discovered that if they removed fresh eggs from the nest, hens would continue laying them. Records show that the ancient Indians then domesticated jungle fowl in at least 3,200 BC, and the Egyptians and Chinese began using eggs as food in 1,400 BC.

Dogs figured out eggs are a delicious, nutritious food *long* before that. Like their wolf ancestors, when ancient, undomesticated dogs hunted for food, they scarfed up birds and the eggs in their nests. By medieval times, dogs were considered companion animals, so their owners fed them scraps of meat, and—when they were sick—more nutritionally complex food like buttered eggs.

Eggs contain all ten essential amino acids dogs need for muscle growth and regeneration—plus taurine, an amino acid cats need in abundance because they can't synthesize it from food. Eggs are rich in antioxidants, especially lutein and zeaxanthin, which protect the eyes from age-related eye conditions like cataracts. In fact, the lutein and zeaxanthin found in eggs may be more bioavailable than the same antioxidants in plant sources. Eggs are also a potent source of choline, a nutrient crucial to the production

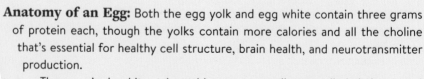

Anatomy of an Egg: Both the egg yolk and egg white contain three grams of protein each, though the yolks contain more calories and all the choline that's essential for healthy cell structure, brain health, and neurotransmitter production.

Those squiggly white stringy things on egg yolks are called chalazae, and they're great to eat. These little protein springs suspend the yolk inside the shell, and the fresher the egg, the more prominent the chalazae. Don't freak out if you spot specks of blood inside an egg. The blood comes from tiny vessels in the yolk, and it is perfectly okay to consume.

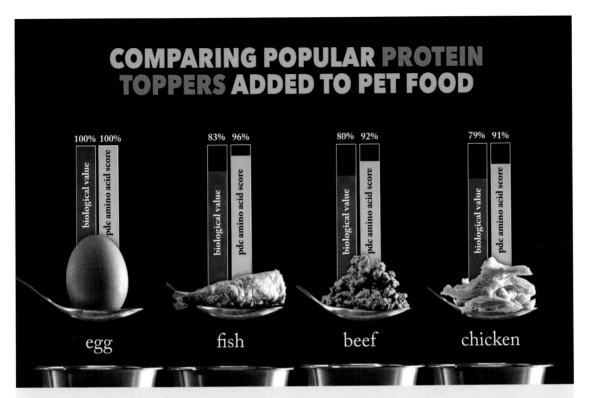

COMPARING POPULAR PROTEIN TOPPERS ADDED TO PET FOOD

egg — 100% biological value, 100% pdc amino acid score

fish — 83% biological value, 96% pdc amino acid score

beef — 80% biological value, 92% pdc amino acid score

chicken — 79% biological value, 91% pdc amino acid score

Eggs Win the Protein Race: There are a few ways to measure the bioavailability of a protein. These include:

- **Biological Value:** A percentage measure of how well the body can absorb protein. A protein with 100 percent biological value means that every single amino acid that makes up the protein is present in a way the body can metabolize it. If the percentage is lower, the protein may lack essential amino acids the body needs.

- **Protein-Digestibility Amino Acid Score (PDCAAS):** A measure of how well a protein can meet the body's amino acid needs. Animal proteins score high, while plant proteins come in a bit lower.

Compared to meat from chicken, beef, and fish, eggs win!

of the neurotransmitter acetylcholine in the brain, which aids brain function and memory, and may help treat and even prevent "doggy dementia." Low choline levels are also associated with liver and heart disease, and choline promotes DNA synthesis, fat metabolism, muscle health, and cell structure. While most commercial pet foods add supplemental choline, a tremendous amount is still lost when that food is cooked, processed, or frozen. Eggs are the ideal choline source!

For maximum nutrition, try to choose pasture-raised eggs. Happy, well-nourished chickens that spend time outside produce eggs that may show a hundredfold increase in carotenoids, including beta-carotene and lutein, and higher levels of omega-3 fatty acids and vitamin E. Feed your dog eggs fol-lowing the serving suggestion on page 48, as a topper, treat, or a part of their complete and balanced meals. Their brains, bones, muscles, organs, and taste buds will thank you.

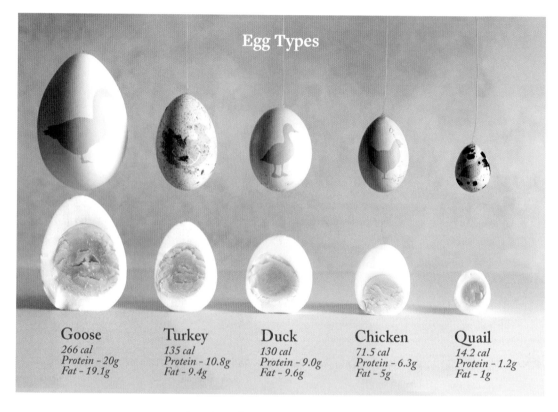

Egg Types

Goose	Turkey	Duck	Chicken	Quail
266 cal	135 cal	130 cal	71.5 cal	14.2 cal
Protein - 20g	Protein - 10.8g	Protein - 9.0g	Protein - 6.3g	Protein - 1.2g
Fat - 19.1g	Fat - 9.4g	Fat - 9.6g	Fat - 5g	Fat - 1g

To Cook or Not to Cook?

Wild dogs throughout history consumed eggs raw. We serve them that way most of the time, too, because raw eggs contain between 20–33 percent more omega-3s, choline, vitamin D, DHA, biotin, and zinc than cooked varieties. Cooking has also been found to reduce the vitamin A concentra-tion in eggs by around 17–20 percent and the number of some antioxidants by 6–18 percent.

A lot of people believe raw eggs should be avoided because of salmonella, which may cause food poisoning in humans. That's not a concern for dogs; salmonella is a natural inhabitant of their GI tracts. Others worry about the fact that egg whites contain avidin, a protein that binds with vitamin B7 (biotin) and may prevent its absorption. The good news is that eggs contain *plenty* of biotin, so any that's lost because of avidin is replaced almost immediately.

If you do want to cook your eggs, aim for

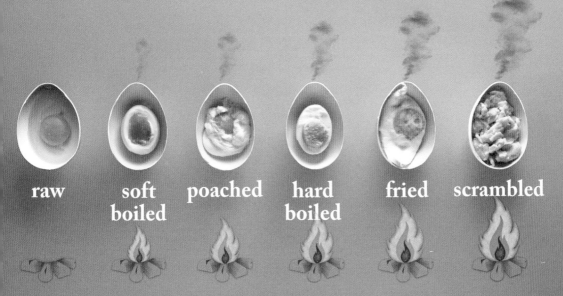

raw   soft boiled   poached   hard boiled   fried   scrambled

shorter cooking times. We like soft boiling because the water, eggshell, and egg white protect the yolk, while the egg white gets just enough heat to remove B7-destroying avidin.

Poaching also preserves over 80 percent of the vitamin D found in eggs (as compared to losing 61 percent when baked for forty minutes).

raw

3 min

5 min

8 min

10 min

12 min

Eggshell Calcium Powder

Eggshells are rich in calcium carbonate—about 800 milligrams!—and the slippery membrane that lines the inside of the shell is loaded with collagen, elastin, protein, hyaluronic acid, glucosamine, and chondroitin, which provide fantastic joint support. Supplementing with eggshell membranes has even been shown to reduce joint pain by 72.5 percent.

Add this easy-to-make calcium powder to your dog's fresh, homemade food that calls for eggshell powder. (It's not necessary to add calcium to commercial pet food that already contains calcium.)

1. Preheat oven to 300°F.

2. Rinse eggshells under cold water.

3. Place eggshells in oven-safe cookware.

4. Cook 5–7 minutes or until dry.

5. Once cool, grind in a blender, food processor, or coffee grinder until you have a fine powder.

6. Store in airtight container in a dry, cool place for up to two months (we like the freezer).

Storing Eggs

Unless you keep chickens or know exactly where your eggs came from, refrigerate your eggs. The USDA requires American eggs to be washed and/or sanitized, which removes the natural coating that protects them from infection. This is why American eggs must be refrigerated. You can store raw eggs from three to five weeks, and hard-boiled ones will keep in the refrigerator for a week.

In addition, you can freeze your cooked eggs for up to one year. Just don't wrap them directly in plastic wrap—it can leach endocrine-disrupting chemicals into food. Raw eggs can be frozen whole for a month, and we love cracking them into muffin tins, then freezing them for future use.

Freshness Tests: Eggshells have up to seventeen thousand tiny pores, and over time they absorb air. The older the egg, the more buoyant it will be in water, and fresh eggs will sink to the bottom of a glass. Fresh eggs also have cloudy whites, whereas older eggs have clear whites. Always rely on the sniff test for freshness; if a freshly cracked egg smells rotten, it is, so throw it out.

Pastured Yolk versus Factory-Farmed Yolk: The difference between pasture-raised eggs and factory farm eggs is written all over the yolk.

Light-yellow yolk: Hens consumed barley and wheat-based poultry feed.

Medium-yellow yolk: Hens consumed alfalfa and corn-based poultry feed.

Dark-yellow yolk: Hens consumed living foods, including green vegetables with a spectrum of healthy plant pigments.

Forever Food:
Sardines (and Other Small Fish)

Sardines are small fish that pack a powerful protein punch. Rich with cancer-fighting omega-3s and vitamins D and B12, as well as the longevity-boosting, heart-happy molecule coenzyme Q10 (CoQ10), sardines are awesome additions to any bowl.

Serving Suggestions: Feed one fresh sardine (they're bigger) or two canned sardines for every twenty pounds of weight, two or three times per week.

There's a lot we can learn from poop. Five-thousand-year-old dog feces discovered in Slovenia was determined to be full of fish and three-hundred-year-old dog poop from Alaska's permafrost proved that sled dogs were fed chinook, sockeye, and coho salmon. In both cases, these fish-filled meals were consistent with the diet of humans at the time. Clearly, dogs have not just eaten fish for millennia, but they've shared it with their human companions.

Our animals' bodies *need* fish, and one type—the sardine—is among our favorite Forever Foods.

Sardines get their name from Sardinia, the Italian "Blue Zone" island that includes the highest proportion of men over the age of one hundred in the world. The name fits them to a T because these little fish hold the secret to longevity—for humans *and* pets. They are one of the top sources of omega-3 fatty acids DHA and EPA, both of which decrease inflammation, prevent and fight cancer, and treat skin allergies, coat problems, dry eyes, valve disorders of the heart, and osteoarthritis in dogs

and cats. Increasing DHA and EPA intake can prevent DNA damage in heart cells, and healthy, undamaged cells are one of the hallmarks of longevity. DHA also improves cognitive performance in aging dogs and, in cats, reduces inflammation markers and protects the kidneys. Sardines are also one of earth's richest sources of coenzyme Q10, an antioxidant that aids mitochondria (for energy production) and can slow the progression of heart disease. One recent study demonstrates that CoQ10 increases life span, and another shows that humans who take CoQ10 not only live longer, but live *better*, with fewer days in the hospital.

Finally, our carnivorous companions need protein for their muscles, connective tissue, skin, hair, joints, and nails, and sardines provide a whopping four grams of protein per sardine. This makes them excellent additions for animals eating dry food, aging animals that are losing muscle mass, and athletic pets.

Shrimp

Taurine 31 *mg/100g*

EPA + DHA 61 *mg/100g*

Oysters

Taurine 69.8 *mg/100g*

EPA + DHA 688 *mg/100g*

Mussels

Taurine 665 *mg/100g*

EPA + DHA 441 *mg/100g*

Scallops

Taurine 827 *mg/100g*

EPA + DHA 150 *mg/100g*

Sardines

Taurine 147 *mg/100g*

EPA + DHA 2760 *mg/100g*

Herring

Taurine 154.4 *mg/100g*

EPA + DHA 1571 *mg/100g*

Mackerel

Taurine 207 *mg/100g*

EPA + DHA 2298 *mg/100g*

Salmon

Taurine 130 *mg/100g*

EPA + DHA 1962 *mg/100g*

Try Other Small Fish: While we love sardines, many types of small fish and shellfish confer similar health benefits in terms of DHA, EPA, and taurine. We often call these "clean fish" because of their low toxic load. Try unbrined anchovies (no added salt), smelt, herring, minnows, mussels, shrimp, and more. A study discovered that people who ate fish at least twice a week (as opposed to never in the past two years) reduced their risk of death *from any cause* by 42 percent! What's good for people is good for pets, so feed your furry friend fish.

Sardines vs. Fish Oil Supplements: While there are benefits to supplementing with fish oil, feeding sardines is superior for its cardiovascular benefits. Fish oil supplements may not as effectively prevent cardiovascular issues, including strokes, heart disease, and arrythmia, and many fish oil supplements are processed using solvents and high heat, which can oxidize their fatty acids and create harmful by-products.

Fresh or Canned?

We recommend using fresh sardines if you can find them. However, both fresh and canned sardines offer health benefits, as long as the canned variety are packed in water (as opposed to salt or brine). Here are a few additional differences:

If you choose canned, look for BPA-free cans (BPA is added to cans to prevent corroding, but it can act as an endocrine disruptor). Always rinse the sardines to remove excess salt. Finally, canned sardine bones are soft and bendable, so they are not considered a choking hazard for most dogs. However, if you're cooking up fresh sardines or have concerns about bones, mash them with a fork and remove bones prior to serving.

Canned	Fresh

Typically $1.50–$3 per four-ounce can	May be slightly more expensive, up to $1/ounce
At stores everywhere	Some grocery stores or fish markets may not have them
High heat required for canning. This reduces vitamins and minerals (including vitamin B1 by 75 percent, vitamin B2 by 51 percent, vitamin B3 by 34 percent, vitamin B6 by 50 percent, and vitamin B12 by 38 percent)	No heat process applied
May contain added salt	No salt

Toxins and Sustainability

Large fish like tuna and swordfish are often contaminated with heavy metal toxins, including mercury. Sardines and other small, clean fish don't live long enough to accumulate the environmental burden of larger fish. For example, sardines dine on plankton, which makes their mercury content *the lowest of any fish*. This is good news for your dog's cardiovascular and nervous systems, GI tract, and kidneys, which high levels of mercury can damage. Try to buy ethically caught seafood and support seafood companies and brands with third-party sustainability certification (such as the Marine Stewardship Council).

Forever Food:
Dandelions

The difference between a weed and a flower is perspective, and we think dandelions are the greatest flowers on earth! They're full of prebiotic fiber that's good for the gut, as well as polyphenols that cleanse the liver, keep the bloodstream healthy, prevent inflammation, and help manage chronic diseases like diabetes. Dandelions are also a powerful topical agent for painful wounds or dry, cracked paws.

Serving Suggestions:
Dried root, leaves, and flowers: ¼ teaspoon for every ten pounds
Fresh root, leaves, and flowers: ½ teaspoon for every ten pounds
Serve twice daily over food.

For as long as dogs have roamed through fields and meadows, they've eaten dandelions. Once native only to Europe and Asia, some historians speculate that the fluffy, gray seeds that make up *Taraxacum officinale* came to America on the first explorers' ships. Soon, settlers began to grow them as food and use them in medicine.

Dogs have known about dandelions' golden goodness all along. As they've munched bright yellow flowers, they've received a healthy dose of lecithin (for memory, immune support, and cellular health), polyphenols (which prevent inflammation), and antioxidants (to protect their cells). They've enjoyed the hearty leaves, which are jam-packed with vitamins C and K and the all-important electrolyte potassium (for muscles, nerves, and fluid balance). They also protect the liver by stimulating bile production and increasing circulation. The roots are

fantastic, too; they can obliterate both colon and gastric cancer cells—in as little as forty-eight hours.

One of dandelion's most important nutritional functions, though, is its role in supporting the microbiome. One of the bacterial species that's terrific for dogs and cats is *A. muciniphila*, which protects the lining of the gut and, in turn, prevents diarrhea and irritable bowel syndrome and may combat obesity. Bacteria need to eat, and *A. muciniphila* loves to feast on fructooligosaccharides and inulin, two prebiotics dandelions contain in abundance.

The Delightful, Delicious, and Nutritious Dandelion

All parts of the dandelion are edible. Let your dog loose in a dandelion-filled spring lawn—as long as it's free of pesticides and other lawn chemicals—or buy dandelion greens from your grocery store or farmers' market. Rinse and dry them, then sauté, feed raw, or cook them in a complete and balanced meal your dog will love.

According to nutritionists, dandelions are one of the top five most nutritious plants in the world. Compared to broccoli, spinach, and carrots—the top three vegetable ingredients in commercial pet food—dandelions have more vitamins E, K, B1, B6, choline, calcium, and iron. And they're often free, as they grow in many parts of the world.

Dandelions for Topical Treatments: Dandelions are powerful if used topically. They are emollient (for soothing the skin), anodyne (for relieving pain), and vulnerary (for healing wounds). The flowers make excellent salves and oils for treating dry, cracked paws and hot spots, cleaning ears, and more. Turn to page 270 for healing oil and salve recipes.

flower

leaf

Caffeic acid - *Antioxidative & immunostimulatory*

Chicoric acid - *Immunostimulatory & anti-hyperglycemic*

Chlorogenic acid - *Antioxidative & immunostimulatory*

Chrysoeriol - *Anticancer, anti-inflammatory, antibacterial, antifungal, & neuroprotective*

Luteoline 7-O-glucoside - *Antioxidant*

Monocaffeoyltartaric acid - *Antioxidant*

α-amyrin - *Anti-inflammatory & antioxidant*

ß-sitosterol - *Anti-inflammatory*

Chicoric acid - *Immunostimulatory & anti-hyperglycemic*

Monocaffeoyltartaric acid - *Antioxidant*

Quercetine glycosides - *Antioxidant*

Sesquiterpene lactones - *Anti-inflammatory & antimicrobial properties*

Stigmasterol - *Anti-tumor effect*

root

11ß,13-dihydrolactucin - *Anti-inflammatory*

Caffeic acid - *Antioxidative & immunostimulatory*

Chicoric acid - *Immunostimulatory & anti-hyperglycemic*

Ixerine - *Anti-inflammatory & antimicrobial*

Monocaffeoyltartaric acid - *Antioxidant*

Taraxasterol - *Antihyperglycemic & anti-inflammatory*

Taraxacolide ß-D-glucoside - *Anti-inflammatory, antimicrobial & hypolipidemic properties*

Taraxinic acid ß-D-glucoside - *Anti-inflammatory & antimicrobial properties*

Tetrahydroridentin B - *Anti-inflammatory & anti-microbial properties*

Flowers

Benefits	Rich in antioxidants and antimicrobial properties. Also a powerful anti-inflammatory.
Harvesting	Pick them when they're flowering, not when they are fluffy and seeding.
Cooking and Feeding	Blanch them in hot water for one minute to remove the bitter taste.
Storing	Wash and dry thoroughly and store them in the refrigerator. Store in the freezer in an airtight container for 2–3 months, or dehydrate and store them in a cool, dry place for up to 3 months.

Leaves

Benefits	Rich in vitamins and minerals, act as a diuretic, boost digestion
Harvesting	Pick the leaves before the flowers bloom. After flowering, the leaves may be too bitter.
Cooking and Feeding	Blanch them in hot water for one minute to remove the bitter taste. Can be fed fresh—we love to mince them and use them as a topper.
Storing	Rinse what you pick and allow it to dry, then freeze or dehydrate. If you plan to eat the leaves within 2–3 days, store them in the refrigerator in a sealed container.

Roots

Benefits	Good for the stomach and liver. Also a powerful diuretic.
Harvesting	Wait until fall to harvest them.
Cooking and Feeding	Wash and boil them for tea. Or boil until tender and feed them whole (or chopped).
Storing	Wash and store them in the refrigerator, freeze them in a sealed container, or dehydrate them. Use within 3 months.

Forever Foods:
Sprouts and Herbs

Crunchy, nutrient-dense, and packed with gut-friendly goodness, sprouts are tiny veggies that make a big impact. The same goes for herbs; even just a sprinkle can add major nutritional benefits to your pet's diet. You can cultivate herbs and sprouts if you live in a closet-sized city apartment, or if you have acres of fertile soil to your name. Sprouts and herbs are versatile, delicious, and healing from the inside out. You'll see sprouts and herbs in many of our recipes, but thanks to their tiny size and big health benefits, they can be easily added to any meal, snack, or lick mat.

Serving Suggestions: Feed a teaspoon of chopped sprouts per twenty pounds of your dog's weight, ½ teaspoon for cats, per day.

Sprouts

Sprouts are cancer and chronic disease fighting cruciferous vegetables that are richer in vitamins, minerals, fiber, and phytochemicals than their grown-up versions. For example, compared to broccoli, broccoli sprouts contain fifty to one hundred times the amount of sulforaphane. Germinating sprouts also increases vitamins A precursors, B, C, and E by 20 percent to 9,000 percent, and eating a small portion of sprouts daily reduces inflammation—a major cause of chronic illness—in less than two months.

Benefits
- Contains fiber, vitamin C, glucoraphanin, and sulforaphane
- Fights cancer, reduces inflammation, and detoxifies the body from carcinogens, heavy metals, Maillard reaction products (unwanted by-products in most pet food from high heat processing), and mycotoxins

Notes
- A single dose of broccoli sprouts given to dogs increased the amount of sulforaphane in their bloodstream, which helps their white blood cells fight cancer growth.

Benefit
- Full of beta-carotene, an antioxidant

Notes
- Slightly peppery, so finicky dogs may not love them
- Arugula is sold as microgreens, not sprouts (see page 68 for more information on microgreens).

Benefits
- Contains choline, chlorophyll, amino acids, and polyphenols
- Promotes gut health, reduces inflammation, and is antibacterial

Notes
- Basil is sold as microgreens, not sprouts (see page 68 for more on microgreens).

Benefits
- Contains chlorophyll, vitamin E, selenium, zinc, and manganese
- Promotes eye health and reduces age-related diseases

Notes
- Dogs love the nutty flavor.

Benefits
- Full of anthocyanins, folate, vitamins C and E, and the amino acid L-glutamine
- Prevents cancer, promotes eye health, reduces inflammation in the GI tract

Notes
- If your dog is not accustomed to eating cabbage, start with a small, cooked portion. Then slowly increase the amount as their gut terrain adjusts, eventually cooking it less until their body accepts raw cabbage without the gassy side effects.

Benefits
- Contains vitamin C, B vitamins, folate
- Promotes cardiovascular health, protects against carcinogens

Notes
- Slightly peppery, so finicky dogs may not love them

Benefits
- Contains the antioxidants beta-carotene, zeaxanthin, and lutein
- Declared by the CDC as a "Powerhouse Veggie" most strongly associated with reduced chronic disease

Notes
- 100 percent nutrient-dense!
- Watercress is sold as microgreens, not sprouts (see page 68 for more information on microgreens).

Benefits
- Full of phytochemicals and the antioxidant resveratrol (one hundred times more than red wine!)
- Anti-inflammatory and anticancer

Notes
- Buy shelled, whole, raw organic Spanish peanuts for sprouting. Sprouting dramatically reduces the fat content. Excellent for training treats.

How to Grow Sprouts

What You'll Need

Sprouting seeds of your choice

Measuring spoons

2-quart glass jar

Optional: sanitizing agent
(apple cider vinegar)

Cheesecloth and rubber band or sprouting
lid with screen

1. Add 1–7 tablespoons of sprouting
   seeds (every tablespoon of seeds is
   approximately 1 cup of sprouts) to glass
   jar.

2. Fill the jar with filtered water, covering
   the seeds, plus 1 inch.

3. *Optional*: Add sanitizing agent
   (1 tablespoon apple cider vinegar).
   Let sit for 10 minutes, then rinse *very
   well* with fresh filtered water. (We rinse
   up to 7 times.)

4. If you sanitized your seeds, add filtered
   water again, covering the seeds plus
   1 inch.

5. Soak seeds for 8 hours or overnight.

6. Drain water from the jar, then add fresh
   filtered water through the lid and swirl
   the seeds to rinse them. Drain the water
   again and rest the jar at an angle, so any
   remaining water can evaporate.

7. Rinse and drain the seeds at least twice
   a day for 3–5 days.

8. When your seeds have sprouted and
   are an inch or so in length (usually the
   third or fourth day), place the jar on a
   sunny windowsill. Watch the sprouts turn
   green!

9. While sprouts are still in the jar, rinse
   them to remove the seed hulls, then
   drain them thoroughly.

10. Refrigerate in jar and use within 5 days.

11. *Optional*: Chop up sprouts prior to
    feeding. This triggers an enzymatic
    reaction that results in the production
    of more of the anticancer compound
    sulforaphane!

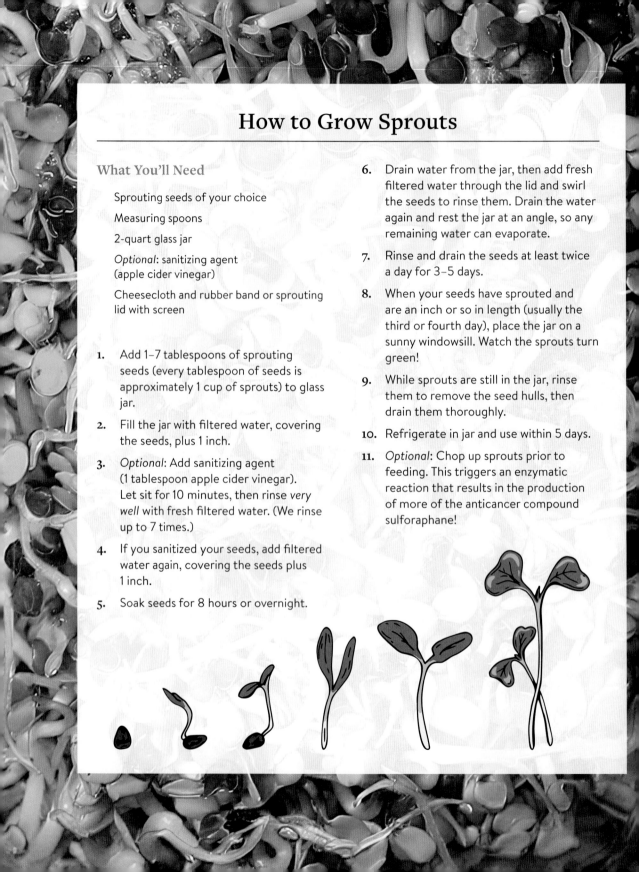

Sanitizing Sprouts: All seeds and peanuts are prone to mold contamination, so mycotoxins can be a concern when you're growing sprouts. However, sanitizing seeds with apple cider vinegar prior to sprouting has been shown to significantly reduce fungal growth (without affecting quality).

Sprouts and AGEs

While studies show that the sulforaphanes in sprouts—especially broccoli sprouts—are highly effective at removing the heavy metals and mycotoxins that are found in abundance in processed dog food, perhaps their most significant job is that they can remove more AGEs than any other food.

AGE stands for "advanced glycation end products," and they are the result of chemical reactions that occur both in the body and during cooking, whenever sugar binds with protein in a warm environment (a process called glycation). AGEs are big and unwieldy and accumulate in tissues, eventually creating structural changes that impair healthy body functions. AGE consumption is linked to chronic inflammation; oxidative stress; slow tissue repair; kidney, heart, and pancreas damage; and cognitive impairment.

Glycation is abundant during pet food processing, and as cooking temperatures increase, the number of AGEs created in food products skyrockets. Canned and kibble pet food have the highest number of AGEs, and raw pet foods have the least, because no heating occurs during manufacturing. One research group found AGE consumption to be 122 times higher in a dog's daily diet, compared to average human AGE intake.

To reduce the AGEs in your pet's diet, stay away from ultra-processed pet food and try cooking homemade diets at lower temperatures (slow cookers/Crock-Pots are great for keeping AGE levels low) and the shortest duration of time you can. In addition, incorporating broccoli sprouts into your pet's meals can protect them against the damaging effects of AGEs. The sulforaphanes in sprouts activate enzymes that shield the cells from AGEs, so add a pinch of these little gems to every bowl of food, regardless of what type of food you're feeding.

Microgreens versus Sprouts

Though they're often confused, there's a difference between microgreens and sprouts. Sprouts are seeds that have germinated in water, and they will eventually become a full-fledged plant if you let them grow. Microgreens are the first leaves that show up on a plant, and they are grown in soil, not water. While sprouts sprout in a few days, microgreens take up to a week or more.

Herbs and Spices

The first recorded use of herbs for healing was in 3,000 BC by the Egyptians and Chinese, but we know that Indigenous cultures used herbs in healing rituals long before that. Dogs were right there, too; for as long as they've snacked on outdoor plants (read: *forever*), they've been gobbling up herbs for good health.

Learning what herbs and spices your animals like, love, and loathe is also a fun way to know their food preferences. And remember, taste preferences change over time. Just like people, some animals enjoy cilantro, and some hate it. Look for organically grown herbs, and always check the expiration dates. Then add a "whisper" (the tiniest micro-pinch or dash) of a new herb to a meatball or a smear of plain yogurt, ricotta, or cottage cheese on a lick mat and discover how excited or annoyed your animals are about tasting a new herb. You'll not only be supercharging your Forever Food recipe's flavor, you'll also be giving your best friend boundless health-boosting benefits. (Just don't feed chives or nutmeg—see below.)

Serving Suggestions: If you choose dried herbs, use one shake for every ten pounds of weight, per day. For fresh herbs, use ¼ teaspoon per twenty pounds of weight, per day.

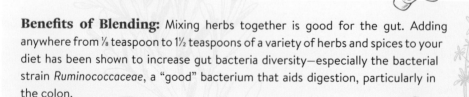

Benefits of Blending: Mixing herbs together is good for the gut. Adding anywhere from ⅛ teaspoon to 1½ teaspoons of a variety of herbs and spices to your diet has been shown to increase gut bacteria diversity—especially the bacterial strain *Ruminococcaceae*, a "good" bacterium that aids digestion, particularly in the colon.

Avoid These Herbs

- **Chives:** Though they're commonly believed to be a part of the onion family, they're only close cousins. However—like leeks and onions—they contain a compound called n-propyl disulfide that can cause a breakdown of red blood cells and lead to anemia.

- **Nutmeg:** Nutmeg contains a compound called myristicin, which can cause GI upset.

Freezing Herbs: Too many herbs and not enough time to dry them? Try freezing.

- Remove the thick stems from your herbs.
- Place leaves flat on parchment paper, freeze them, then transfer to a silicone storage bag and store in the freezer for up to a year.

   Or

- Remove thick stems from your herbs.
- Finely chop herbs with a knife, or, if you have a lot of herbs, use a food processor.
- Pack chopped herbs into an ice cube tray, adding olive oil, black cumin seed oil, filtered water, or broth to make removal easier.

Herbs for Health

Recipes throughout this book will feature herbs as ingredients, but feel free to supercharge any meal with a sprinkling of these herbs. Note: while essential oils are extracted from many herbs, essential oil extracts are much more potent than fresh or dried herbs and should not be used as a replacement.

Curly Parsley

- Contains myricetin, an antioxidant that slows the growth of breast cancer cells
- Contains a flavonoid called apigenin that also suppresses the growth of breast cancer cells
- A particularly rich source of vitamin K, which is essential for bone and blood health
- Contains polyacetylene, which reduces the carcinogenic effects of aflatoxins, a mold by-product often found in pet food

Turmeric

- Its active ingredient, curcumin, suppresses the release of cytokines (substances released by immune cells), which helps kill cancer stem cells and has anti-inflammatory effects on dogs with arthritis.
- Antioxidant, blocks the action of free radicals
- May increase levels of BDNF, a protein associated with reduced rates of brain disorders

Rosemary

- Contains a polyphenol called carnosic acid that protects the brain from damage due to free radicals
- Contains carnosic acid and another polyphenol, rosmarinic acid, which may suppress signaling molecules that cause cancer
- Increases glutathione levels in dogs and has a positive effect on pancreatic function

Cilantro

- Helps the body flush out sodium, which regulates blood pressure
- Helps control blood sugar by promoting the enzyme activity that eliminates sugar from the blood
- Helps eliminate mercury and lead from the body

Cumin

- Improves digestion by increasing the activity of the enzymes amylase, protease, lipase, and phytase
- Antimicrobial against gram positive and gram negative bacteria and yeast
- Decreases insulin levels, which helps control diabetes

Cinnamon

- Inhibits the formation of AGEs
- Contains a compound called cinnamaldehyde (which gives it flavor and odor) that builds collagen and helps joints
- Contains antioxidants that protect the cardiovascular system by reducing oxidative stress
- Contains polyphenols that prevent neurodegenerative diseases like doggy dementia

Cloves (grind, do not feed whole)

- Inhibits the formation of AGEs
- Rich in manganese, which helps joints and ligaments
- Contains a bioactive compound called eugenol that inhibits inflammation from cytokines
- Eugenol also improves liver function by inhibiting the formation of cells that form cirrhosis

Basil

- Contains eugenol, which relaxes blood vessels, lowers blood pressure, and helps regulate blood glucose levels
- Its compounds eugenol, citronellol, and linalool inhibit cytokines and gene expression, which prevents inflammation.

Oregano

- Its chemical compounds thymol and carvacol are potent antioxidants that inhibit the oxidation of fatty acids, which prevents cell damage.
- Demonstrates antibacterial properties against twenty-three bacteria that can lead to infection

Thyme

- Contains baicalein, which induces dog bone cancer cell death
- Contains a phenol called thymol that breaks down the cell membranes of pathogens, making it antimicrobial

Ginger

- Consuming ginger relieves the inflammation associated with muscle pain.
- Helps decrease levels of inflammatory molecules (eicosanoids) that can lead to the development of colon cancer
- Contains oils and phenolic compounds that help reduce nausea

TREATS
and
TOPPERS

P et treats have long been associated with empty calories, carb-heavy fillers, and a wad of additives that do more harm to your pet than good. Most mammals love snacks, but dogs and cats don't need junk food, so we've crafted the following nutritionally rich treats and toppers that—along with CLTs—will *replace the 10 percent nutrient-starved scraps, kibble, and treats you may have been feeding your pet.*

Treats can serve a purpose—to reward your pet for a job well done or to reinforce good behavior while training—so continue using them this way. Try to steer clear of giving treats because your pet is lonely or bored, because you think they're cute, or because they're hanging around the kitchen. Keep your treats small to avoid a blood sugar spike—the size of a pea or blueberry is ideal—and note what it is your dog responds to. Do they love the flavor of carrots? Stick with the carrot treats and toppers to start. Are chicken hearts doing it for them? That's great! Keep it up! Then branch out into similar but new flavors they might enjoy, and continue on this healthy snacking trend, sequentially trying new treats, even ones your beloved refused last month.

New Foods Provide Enrichment:

Animals who consume the same food every day miss out on the opportunity to try new textures and flavors. Imagine eating cereal daily, then being offered a delectable, warm, homemade stew. Trying new foods provides an enriching sensory experience for our animals.

Double the enrichment value by offering a variety of foods in a novel presentation: fill each individual cup in an empty egg carton, using new or familiar foods, and varying taste, texture, and even temperature to elevate feeding time to a total sensory experience.

Jerkies and Dehydrated Snacks

Whether you make it from vegetables or meat, jerky is flavorful, concentrated nutrition. Use jerky as a training treat, a reward, or a way to pack in a quick nutrient boost. We've held off suggesting ingredient sizes because you may want to make a small portion of jerky—or you may want to make a lot. All jerkies or dehydrated meats and vegetables can be stored in an airtight container in the refrigerator for a month or the freezer for up to three months. Thaw prior to feeding.

Spotlight on Organ Meats: Organ meats are powerful ancestral sources of protein, and 4,500-year-old fossilized poop, found only a few miles from Stonehenge, reveals that dogs ate internal organs—oftentimes raw or undercooked by their people. Organ meats are also full of vitamins, minerals, and fatty acids, and dogs fed organ meats have significantly lower rates of skin allergies in adulthood.

Use the "paw principle" to determine how much organ meat your dog can snack on per day. The size of one of their paws (width, length, and depth) is an appropriate amount of organ meat treats/toppers or add-ins. Feed a variety of organ meats to diversify your pet's intake of a broad spectrum of minerals, including:

- **Liver:** Nature's richest source of copper, plus iron and vitamins A, D, E, and K. Some people think that eating liver is toxic to pets, but it's not. Liver *filters out* toxins rather than *storing them*. Instead, it stores nutrients! However, if you feed commercial pet food that contains both liver and a copper supplement, you should minimize feeding additional liver and choose other organs as toppers and treats.

- **Heart:** A great source of taurine, but feed raw, lightly cooked, or dehydrated because taurine losses increase with heat. Hearts are also full of iron, selenium, zinc, and B vitamins, and are one of the best nutritional sources of CoQ10.

- **Kidneys:** Rich in protein, folate, omega-3 fatty acids, and diamine oxidase (DAO), the enzyme that breaks down histamine (excellent for allergic animals). Beef kidneys and hearts also contain more alpha-lipoic acid (ALA) than any other food!

- **Fresh tripe (stomach):** Rich in probiotics, prebiotics, and minerals, including manganese, iron, potassium, zinc, copper, and selenium. Tripe sold in the meat section of grocery stores or that's been canned or dried has few nutritional benefits. Seek it out fresh (aka "green") from specialty raw food retailers or local farmers.

- **Brain:** Richer in DHA than fish! Steer clear of raw cow and venison brains, which can cause prion disease and lead to neurological conditions.

Meat Jerky

Meat: Boneless chicken breast, rabbit loin, lean cut of beef (such as sirloin), liver, turkey breast, lamb loin, or lean pork

Fresh or dried herbs to taste (ginger, turmeric, rosemary, cumin, basil, or others)

Pinch of sesame seeds, chia, or flaxseeds

1 tablespoon coconut oil, pineapple juice, or raw honey

1 teaspoon ground turmeric root, "coconut aminos" (coconut-derived soy sauce substitute), or almond butter

Optional toppings: Dress up your jerky as we did—or experiment with whatever you like.

In an oven:

1. Preheat oven to 170°F.

2. If using cuts of meat, partially freeze the meat (for approximately 15–20 minutes) to make it easier to slice.

3. Cut off all visible fat. Slice the meat lengthwise into uniform strips, ⅛ to ¼ inch thick. Note: if the meat is thicker than ¼ inch, it takes longer to dehydrate.

4. *Optional:* Sprinkle with herbs or seeds, glazing with oil, juice, or honey and turmeric, almond butter, or coconut aminos.

5. Place pieces in a single layer, spaced 1 inch apart, on a greased metal rack.

6. Place rack on top of a baking sheet to catch drippings.

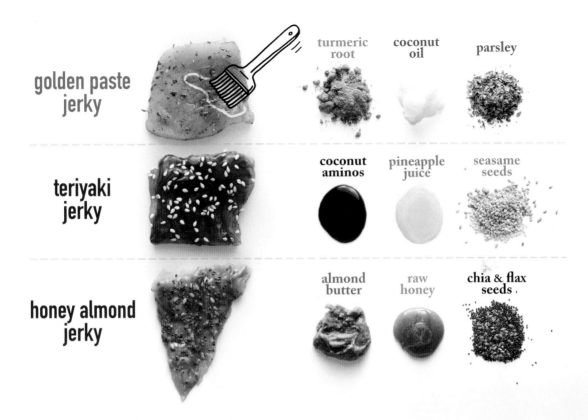

golden paste jerky — turmeric root, coconut oil, parsley

teriyaki jerky — coconut aminos, pineapple juice, seasame seeds

honey almond jerky — almond butter, raw honey, chia & flax seeds

7. Place in oven, then crack door open with a wooden spoon.

8. Cook for five hours or until the meat is crisp and breaks easily, flipping over the strips midway through cooking time.

Note: If the meat is not cooked thoroughly until crisp, it risks spoiling quickly.

In a dehydrator:

1. Follow preparation above (cutting meat, sprinkling or mixing herbs, and glazing).

2. Place meat slices on a lightly greased rack, spaced 1 inch apart.

3. Dehydrate at 160°F for 6–12 hours or until the meat is crisp and breaks easily.

Be Patient with Your Dehydrator: Dehydration times can vary based on the humidity levels in your home, which impact the degree to which food dehydrates. Adjust temperature and cooking times as needed.

Ground Meat Jerky

Meat:

8 ounces lean ground meat
(rabbit, turkey, chicken, beef, bison,
or any novel protein)

3 tablespoons gelatin powder

Optional: your favorite herbs

1. Preheat oven to 200°F.

2. Mix ingredients in a medium bowl until well combined.

3. Press mixture into a flat layer on a parchment paper–lined baking sheet. It should be a thin layer, but not so thin that the paper shows through.

4. Bake for 1 hour.

5. Remove the sheet from the oven and turn the oven off.

6. Lay a second sheet of parchment paper on top of the jerky, then flip the baking sheet over to transfer the jerky to the second sheet.

7. Place the jerky back in the oven (turned off), using a baking sheet under the parchment paper if needed for stability.

8. Let the jerky dry and cool in the oven for 3 hours.

9. Cut into bite-sized strips.

10. For extra-crispy jerky, cook an additional two hours at 160°F.

Dehydrating Broccoli: We cut off the broccoli stems before making jerky because they take a bit longer to dry. Do *not* throw the stems out; they're a highly nutritious ready-to-feed treat, so chop them into bite-sized pieces.

Broccoli is a powerful source of two supermolecules: 3,3'-Diindolylmethane (DIM) and sulforaphane, both of which turn on the body's production of glutathione, an antioxidant whose detox abilities are one of the body's most potent. Broccoli stems have double the amount of sulforaphane compared to florets. (Note: you can't supplement with sulforaphane because it degrades too quickly. Taking it in through food is the way to go.) DIM also helps balance hormones, is anticancer, and clears the body of xenoestrogens, dangerous environmental chemicals that mimic estrogen.

Never microwave your broccoli, because even five minutes reduces the flavonoid (antioxidant) content by a whopping 97 percent.

Fruit and Vegetable Jerky

Dehydrating is a great way to use your leftover fruit and veggies before they go bad. The fact is you can dehydrate almost anything—from bananas to blueberries to broccoli . . . to whatever your pet loves to eat or that fits around their dietary needs and goals. (We'd like to give a special shout-out to dried banana chips, which may be the best training treats on the planet and are great for dogs with sensitive stomachs.) Have a senior with no teeth? Go soft and small. Dieting dogs appreciate small and crunchy, and puppies need micro-rewards (as they're in training 24/7). Feel free to add herbs to your fruit or vegetable jerky, too. Simply brush Manuka honey or black seed oil on the food before you dehydrate it, then sprinkle away.

You may need to adjust cooking directions based on the type of fruit or vegetable you use and how water-dense it is. Foods like bananas take a bit longer to dry out, while apples dehydrate more quickly. Note that the thinner you cut a fruit or vegetable, the faster it will turn into jerky.

In an oven:

1. Preheat oven to 170°F (or lowest setting).

2. Cut food into ¼-inch-thick slices or bite-sized pieces.

3. *For vegetables except for green peppers and mushrooms, blanch first:*

   Bring a pot of filtered water to a rolling boil. Fill a separate bowl or pot with filtered ice water.

   Place the vegetable in the boiling water for three minutes, strain, then place in ice water.

   Strain again and allow to dry.

4. Place slices an inch apart on a greased baking sheet, or a silicone baking mat or parchment paper on a baking sheet.

5. Place in oven, propping door open with a wooden spoon.

6. Bake for about 2–2.5 hours, until dried to desired consistency.

In a dehydrator:

1. Cut food into slices ⅛ inch thick, or desired size for training treats. (For vegetables except for green peppers and mushrooms, blanch first, following directions above.)

2. Dehydrate at 135°F for 12–20 hours, or until crisp.

Manuka-Glazed Chicken Jerky

These Manuka honey treats are good for the gut and delicious, with just the tiniest bit of sweetness.

1 tablespoon coconut oil

1 teaspoon grated, chopped, or food processed herb or spice of your choice
(here we use cinnamon and rosemary)

1 tablespoon raw or Manuka honey

1 chicken breast, pounded flat, sliced into strips or bite-sized pieces

Dash of sesame seeds or other seeds
(hemp, chia, black seeds)

1. Preheat oven to 250°F. Grease a baking dish with one tablespoon coconut oil.

2. Mix herbs and honey in a small bowl.

3. Coat chicken with mixture using a silicone brush, or just spoon the mixture over the chicken.

4. Place the chicken in a single layer in the dish. Sprinkle seeds over the chicken.

5. Bake for 45 minutes or until the chicken is fully cooked and opaque white throughout.

Honey for Health: Manuka honey is produced by bees that have foraged on the flowers of *Leptospermum* trees, more commonly known as the tea tree plant, native to Australia and New Zealand. Manuka honey has much higher antibacterial properties than regular, raw honey, which is why it's also used topically to treat burns, wounds, and antibiotic-resistant skin infections. Orally, it's beneficial for gastrointestinal ulcers, and may be of benefit for irritable bowel syndrome.

Bite-Sized Treats

While almost anything can become a bite-sized treat, these recipes are healthy, enriching ways to make your pet's 10 percent add-ons feel special. All treats can be stored in an airtight container in the refrigerator for three days or the freezer for up to three months. Thaw prior to feeding.

Medication Marbles

Next time you're tempted to buy pill pouches at the pet or grocery store, think again. Commercial pill pouches contain all kinds of unnatural ingredients, including wheat gluten, wheat flour, corn syrup, and vegetable oil, which pets have no need for. If your pet isn't a fan of pills, disguise them in this choline-rich treat!

Yields about 9 small or 4 large marbles

1 egg, shelled

1 teaspoon gelatin

1. If using an oven (rather than a microwave), preheat oven to 250°F.

2. Whisk egg and gelatin to thoroughly combine.

3. Pour liquid into a 2-inch-diameter (or smaller) silicone mold or silicone ice cube tray, using the outer cavities.

4. In an oven, cook for 20–25 minutes.

5. Or, in a microwave, cook on high for 10 seconds, then remove and let cool for 15–20 seconds. Microwave again until egg puffs pull away from the sides of the mold.

6. Let cool, then remove the puffs from the mold.

Pro Tips for Popping Pills: When it's pill time, prepare a second, small and unmedicated treat (preferably your pet's absolute most favorite treat). Immediately after offering the medicated pill pouch, encourage instantaneous swallowing by offering the second delectable morsel.

Have a finicky cat (or dog)? Cream cheese, ricotta cheese, unsweetened applesauce, plain Greek yogurt, meatballs, almond butter, or fresh mozzarella cheese can also help mask medications, supplements, or pills.

beef 'n' cheese pouch

- ⅓ cup **cottage cheese**
- ½ cup **ground meat (raw or cooked)**

pumpkin pouch

- 4 teaspoons **gelatin**
- ½ cup canned or steamed 100% **pumpkin puree**, **heated**

almond pouch

- 5 tablespoons almond meal or flour
- ⅓ cup raw **almond butter**

savory cream cheese pouch

- 2 tablespoons broth
- ¼ cup **cream cheese**
- 1–2 teaspoons coconut or almond flour

Sneaky Easy Pill Pouches

These two- to three-ingredient pill pouches are a breeze to make and great at disguising icky pills.

Yields 8–12 pill pouches, depending on how large you roll the balls

1. Combine ingredients in a small bowl (for recipes requiring heating, let cool to lukewarm).

2. Roll into ½- to 1-inch balls, or whatever size pill pouch you need. If a recipe contains meat or flour, wet your fingers before handling to prevent mixture from sticking to your hands.

3. For the Pumpkin Pouch recipe, refrigerate to firm up before rolling into balls.

4. Insert straw into each ball to create a hole for the pill, the "pouch." When it's medication time: insert pill/capsule or powder into the food pouch, pinch closed, and serve.

Note: If you store pill pouches frozen, thaw prior to inserting pills or powders.

Avocado Deviled Eggs

Avocados are rich in vitamins and minerals including vitamins C and E, folate, fiber, healthy fats for brain function, phytosterols for heart function, and—pound for pound—contain more potassium than bananas. They also contain lipase, an enzyme necessary to digest fats. Have a dog who's prone to high cholesterol and triglycerides, like a schnauzer, collie, or Shetland sheepdog? Eating avocados can also help lower triglyceride levels.

2 hard-boiled eggs, shelled

½ ripe avocado

Optional: broccoli sprouts

Optional: DIY Vitamin/Mineral Greens Powder (see page 127)

1. Slice the eggs in half and place the yolks in a small bowl.

2. Add the avocado flesh to the bowl.

3. Mash together until well combined.

4. *Optional*: Stir in broccoli sprouts—or top the mixture with sprouts after the last step.

5. *Optional*: Dust with a pinch of DIY Vitamin/Mineral Greens Powder.

6. Spoon the avocado/yolk mixture into the egg white wells.

Detox Delights

These yummy meatballs can be served cooked or raw, or you can spread the raw meat on a lick mat or crumble and use as a topper.

Yields 18–30 meatballs, depending on size

1 pound ground beef

½ cup cilantro, minced
(or approximately 500 milligrams milk thistle powder, capsules removed)

¼ cup fresh, unsprayed dandelion greens
(or approximately 500 milligrams dandelion powder, capsules removed)

½ cup any medicinal or culinary mushrooms

Optional: ¼ cup sprouts
(any type)

Note: If you use greens rather than capsules, use a maximum of ¾ cup so the meatballs hold together.

1. Preheat oven to 250°F if serving cooked.

2. Mix all ingredients in a medium bowl.

3. If using in a lick mat or as a topper, you can serve now.

4. If baking, roll into marble-sized meatballs and place on an ungreased baking sheet, silicone baking mat, or parchment paper.

5. Bake for 15 minutes for ½-inch-diameter meatballs, 25 minutes for larger meatballs, or until firm throughout.

Cilantro Is a Mold Buster: Mycotoxin is a toxic mold that infects grains, and commercial dog foods are *full* of them. (In one study, nine out of the twelve dog foods tested contained them!) Mycotoxins can lead to organ disease, immunosuppression, cancer, and more, and while it's best to avoid them entirely, sometimes it's too late. Cilantro can help. This flavorful herb contains polyacetylene, an organic compound that helps detoxify mycotoxins from the body. Cilantro can also chelate heavy metals from the body (something commercial dog food is full of), naturally binding an average of 87 percent of lead, 91 percent of mercury, and 74 percent of aluminum within forty-five days.

Immune Puree

This recipe uses medium-chain triglyceride (MCT) oil—a "good fat" extracted from coconut oil, palm oil, or certain dairy products. MCT oil is antimicrobial and energy-boosting, increases omega-3 levels in the brain, and can improve seizures, behavior, and cognitive function in epileptic dogs. Use this recipe as a meal topper or on a lick mat, or pour into ice molds or a mini muffin tin to freeze. Serve at any temperature, though finicky cats love it warm.

Yields about 1 cup

1. Sauté chopped mushrooms in MCT oil on low heat until reduced (about 1 cup total).

2. Puree the mushroom and oil mixture, then add sprouts and optional salt, and puree until smooth.

3. Pour into molds or mini tins to freeze.

4. Thaw prior to feeding (and warm, if desired).

8 ounces (3 cups) medicinal mushrooms, any type, chopped

2 tablespoons MCT oil

½ cup broccoli sprouts

Optional: tiny pinch of Himalayan salt

Serving Suggestions: Most ice cube trays are one ounce, which is the perfect size for a small dog's daily portion. Extra-small dogs and cats can start with 0.5 ounce/day, medium to large dogs 2 ounces, and XL dogs 3 ounces.

Low-Fat Turkey Bites

Low-fat foods like turkey can be soothing to pets with sensitive stomachs, and fermented foods (such as cottage cheese) can help GI issues even more. Add mushrooms or herbs to this treat for an extra nutritional (and flavor) boost.

Yields 6 regular or 12 mini muffins

½ pound ground 99 percent fat-free turkey

¼ cup canned or steamed squash or pumpkin

¼ cup cottage cheese or unsweetened applesauce (recipe on page 122)

1. Preheat oven to 200°F.
2. Combine all ingredients in a medium bowl.
3. Press mixture into muffin tins, filling cavities ⅓ full.
4. Bake for 35 minutes or until cooked through and firm.
5. Let cool 15 minutes, then remove from muffin tin.

Microbiome Morsels

If your pet is prone to constipation, these fiber-rich morsels can help.

Yields 8–12 morsels, depending on size

½ cup psyllium husk powder

½ cup kefir or plain yogurt

1 cup chicken livers, pureed

1 tablespoon gelatin powder

1. Preheat oven to 250°F.

2. Mix all ingredients in a medium bowl.

3. Drop by teaspoonfuls on greased baking sheet, silicone baking mat, or parchment paper.

4. Bake for 15 minutes until the morsels hold together well.

One of Our Favorite Shrubs: Psyllium is a medicinal shrub with an indigestible husk that's chock-full of beneficial dietary fiber. In powder form, psyllium can be added to toppers or lick mats, or snuck into homemade meals or baked goods like these delicious cookies. Not only will it help with constipation, but, for dogs with colitis, psyllium has been found to shorten the duration of a flare-up by 3½ days over antibiotics.

Meatless Morsels

When animals have leaky gut (dysbiosis) and dietary sensitivities, food allergies can develop. Vets often recommend a break from potentially allergenic protein sources, so this treat is especially good for animals who need a meat-free or lower-protein food.

Yields 10–15 morsels, depending on size

1 cup nonwheat flour
(See our favorites on page 101. If using coconut flour, decrease amount to ⅓ cup.)

2 tablespoons olive oil

1 tablespoon gelatin powder

1 small banana, mashed

1. Preheat oven to 250°F.

2. Combine all ingredients in a medium bowl and stir until thoroughly combined.

3. Roll into ½-inch balls and place on a greased baking sheet, silicone baking mat, or parchment paper.

4. Bake for 40 minutes, or until you can lift these treats off the mat, paper, or baking sheet easily.

Jerusalem Artichoke Chips

Also known as sunchokes, Jerusalem artichokes are terrific tubers rich in inulin. Mild, nutty, and slightly sweet, most pets love these microbiome-building crunchy treats.

Jerusalem artichokes
(as many as desired), sliced approximately
⅛ inch thin

1. Preheat oven to 250°F.
2. Place sliced Jerusalem artichokes on a greased baking sheet, silicone baking mat, or parchment paper.
3. Bake 30 minutes. Remove from oven, flip chips, replace in oven, and bake another 30 minutes.
4. Remove when chips are crisp and golden.

Eat Your Microbes: Healthy soil is essential for a healthy gut, and feeding your pet root vegetables like Jerusalem artichokes is a great way to give them the beneficial microbes they need. The microbiome of the soil and the gut are almost identical, yet toxic food, medications, and an unhealthy environment have caused the diversity of mammals' microbiomes to plummet. Microbes from the soil live on food even after it's washed, so feeding your pet organic root vegetables can contribute to a varied, abundant microbiome. In fact, when we asked Tim Spector, professor of genetic epidemiology and director of the Twins UK Registry at King's College London, what one food he would recommend feeding for a better canine microbiome, he immediately said, "Jerusalem artichokes!"

The Celebration Cake

Celebrate special occasions with this dog-safe decadent treat. We like to boil the sweet potatoes in vegetable broth for a nutrient boost.

½ pound ground beef

1 egg, shelled

½ cup oatmeal
(we use steel-cut organic sprouted oats)

¼ cup shredded cheese

1 large or 2 small sweet potatoes

Blueberries, strawberries, and/or peas to garnish

For the cake:

1. Preheat oven to 220°F.

2. Combine beef, egg, oatmeal, and cheese in a medium bowl, mixing until thoroughly combined.

3. Press the mixture into two mini cake tins or shape into patties approximately 6 inches in diameter and place on an ungreased baking sheet, silicone baking mat, or parchment paper.

4. Bake 2½ hours or until done.

5. Press patties flat as soon as they come out of the oven. Let cool.

For the frosting:

1. While the cake is baking, make the frosting.

2. Peel the sweet potato and cut it into 1-inch chunks.

3. Place the chunks into a medium pan and fill with filtered water or broth until the chunks are covered.

4. Bring to a boil over high heat, then lower to medium-low and cook until soft.

5. Drain the water and set it aside.

6. Mash the sweet potato or use an electric mixer, adding reserved water by the tablespoon until a spreadable consistency is reached.

7. Frost the top of one cake with enough mashed sweet potato to cover, then place the second layer on top. Cover the top and sides of the layered cake with the remaining sweet potato.

8. Place blueberries, cut strawberries, and peas on the cake as desired to decorate.

Sweet Potatoes—Colorful, Nutritious, and Delicious: Choose an orange sweet potato for a beta-carotene boost. Beta-carotene is a powerful antioxidant, and research shows that it can help restore immune responses in older dogs, whose immune systems decline as they age. Purple sweet potatoes are rich in compounds called anthocyanins, which are anti-inflammatory and may help prevent cancer and cognitive decline.

HEY, HEY! IT'S MY
ADOPTION
DAY

Green Banana Biscotti

A savory and delicious biscotti, without all the carbs.

Yields 12–15 biscotti

2 green bananas, peeled

¼ cup plain kefir

1½ cups almond flour

1. Preheat oven to 220°F.

2. Blend all ingredients in a blender or mixer.

3. Pour into one greased 5x7-inch loaf pan or two 3x5-inch mini loaf pans. Smooth the tops with a spatula.

4. Bake for 60–90 minutes (the mini loaves bake faster than the larger one). The loaf is done once it springs back when touched lightly.

5. Remove from oven and let cool for 20 minutes. Lower oven temperature to 200°F.

6. Flip cake onto a cutting board and slice into ½-inch strips.

7. Place the strips on a greased baking sheet, silicone baking mat, or parchment paper and bake again for 30 minutes, or until dry on the top side. Flip over and bake for an additional 30 minutes. Continue flipping every 30 minutes until thoroughly dry.

8. Remove from oven and let cool.

9. Store in a dry, cool place for a week. Freeze up to three months.

Go Green for Gut Health: Unripe (green) bananas are the unsung heroes of gut health. They are high in prebiotics, which positively influence blood sugar control and help increase the production of butyrate, a short-chain fatty acid that is formed when starch ferments in the gut. Butyrate acts as an energy source for colon cells (providing up to 70 percent of their energy!), supports the immune system, and helps reduce inflammation. The greener the bananas you use in recipes and as treats, the lower the sugar and the more healthy, resistant starch and pectin are present, which improves gut health and helps keep blood sugar and insulin low and steady.

If you don't bake your green bananas into a tasty training treat, cut them into bite-sized pieces and feed them according to this schedule:

- **Giant breed dogs:** ½ green banana a day
- **Medium to large breeds:** ¼ green banana a day
- **Small breeds:** ⅛ green banana a day
- **Cats:** 2 teaspoons, mashed, per day

Cookies

These guilt-free, nutritious cookies are the perfect treat to have on hand whenever you want to give your pet a healthy snack. Many of the recipes here involve only three ingredients, and you can store the cookies for one week in the refrigerator or up to three months in the freezer. (Just remember to thaw them completely prior to serving.) We recommend breaking treats into tiny pieces, replacing your store-bought pet cookies or treats with these homemade, fresher options.

Good Old-Fashioned Dog Biscuits

These biscuits are as basic as you can get, with gluten-free buckwheat flour derived from seeds, making it naturally low in starch. Note that we use *Himalayan Tartary* buckwheat flour over regular buckwheat flour for the added health benefits. We love to cut these into fun shapes or bite-sized training treats.

Yields 24 2-inch cookies

3 cups Himalayan Tartary buckwheat flour

1 cup broth (see page 142)

⅓ cup butter, softened

Pinch of salt

1. Preheat oven to 250°F.

2. In a bowl, mix ingredients together with an electric mixer.

3. Using a rolling pin, roll dough to ¼ inch flat on silicone mat.

4. Cut into desired shapes using cookie cutters or a pizza cutter, or punch dough with a straw (if making tiny training treats). Or, if you don't want to roll dough flat, you can create different-sized morsels by hand.

5. Place cookies on a baking sheet lined with a silicone baking mat or parchment paper and bake 10–30 minutes depending on size of treats and desired crunchiness.

Carrot Cake Cookies

Carrots are apiaceous vegetables (along with parsley and fennel . . . to name a few), containing high amounts of plant bioactive phenolic compounds and even acting as antimicrobials. Coupled with pecans—which can improve gut health in dogs—these cookies are nutritional powerhouses.

Yields about 8 cookies

⅔ cup carrots, grated

2 eggs, beaten

¼ cup finely chopped raw, unsalted pecans

¼ cup unsweetened shredded coconut

½ teaspoon cinnamon

1 tablespoon coconut flour

For the frosting: Plain Greek yogurt

1. Preheat oven to 250°F.

2. Combine carrot, eggs, pecans, coconut, and cinnamon in a bowl.

3. Stir in coconut flour and incorporate completely.

4. Drop teaspoon-sized morsels on a parchment-lined baking sheet, flattening the mounds slightly.

5. Bake for 60 minutes or until firm.

6. Let cool completely.

7. "Frost" cookies with a dollop of Greek yogurt (about 1 teaspoon per cookie) and top with any extra shredded coconut, if desired.

Though you can use any type of flour or nut butter in the recipes that call for them, these are our favorites:

Type of Flour		Fiber (per ¼ cup)	Protein (per ¼ cup)	Taste, Texture, or Uses
	Almond	1.99 grams	6 grams	• Has a mild, nutty flavor • Has the highest amount of hard-to-come-by vitamin E, important for healthy cell membranes and eyes
	Himalayan Tartary Buckwheat	4 grams	4 grams	• Has an earthy flavor • Buckwheat is a seed, not a grain, and it's entirely unrelated to wheat (and is naturally gluten-free). • Contains over 100 phytochemicals, and is referred to as a "nutraceutical crop"
	Banana	2.5 grams	1 gram	• Has an earthy flavor • Replacing conventional flour with banana flour greatly increases a recipe's antioxidant power.
	Coconut	10 grams	4 grams	• High in gut-friendly fiber • Has a slight coconut flavor • Has healthy fats, including medium-chain triglycerides (MCTs), which research shows improve brain function in aging dogs

Type of Nut Butter		Risks	Rewards
	Peanut (technically a legume)	Peanuts can harbor mycotoxins, so be sure you choose human-grade peanut butter, which is FDA approved. Never choose peanut butter spread, and be sure it does not contain xylitol, which is toxic to dogs.	Higher in protein and niacin than any other nut butter, and also the cheapest
	Sunflower	High chance of being genetically modified (GMO)	Higher in magnesium and vitamins A and E than any other nut butter
	Walnut	Self-harvested walnuts that have fallen from trees are prone to mycotoxins.	Higher in plant-based omega-3 fatty acids than any other nut butter
	Almond	Highest in the anti-nutrient oxalates (see page 28)	Higher in iron, vitamin E, and fiber than any other nut butter and lower in carbohydrates and saturated fat
	Cashew	May contain other added oils, such as safflower oil, so read labels carefully	Lower in fat than any other nut butter

Ultra-Processed Treats

Ginger Bones

Ingredients -
Ground whole wheat, Corn gluten meal, Cane molasses, Chicken fat, Calcium propionate, Titanium dioxide, White cheese powder, Natural bacon flavor, Iron proteinate, Colors (red 3, Sunset yellow FC, Tartrazine, Brilliant blue FF), Copper proteinate.

chemical that can cause DNA or chromosomal damage.

caused cancer in laboratory animals.

Ingredients -
Pumpkin, coconut flour, eggs, almond butter, MCT oil, baking soda, ginger.

Ginger Bones

Rich in antioxidants, ginger promotes healthy blood circulation, acts as an anti-inflammatory, and can relieve nausea (even complete protection against side effects of chemotherapy). It also contains a substance called [6]-gingerol that activates white blood cells, making ginger a powerful immune booster. We love to tie these cookies to a wreath to make a pawliday gift!

Yields about 36 cookies (using 3.5-inch dog bone cookie cutter)

1 cup pumpkin or any steamed squash

1½ cups coconut flour

4 eggs, shelled

½ cup peanut butter or almond butter

½ cup coconut, MCT, or black seed oil

½ teaspoon baking soda

¼ teaspoon dried ginger (or ½ teaspoon freshly grated)

1. Preheat oven to 250°F.

2. Mix all ingredients well in a medium bowl.

3. Place in freezer for 20 minutes to make dough easier to work with.

4. Roll dough out between two sheets of parchment paper to about ¼-inch uniform thickness.

5. Use a bone-shaped cookie cutter to cut out bones.

6. Transfer the bones to a greased baking sheet, silicone baking mat, or parchment paper, leaving at least 1 inch between them.

7. Bake for 30–45 minutes or until bones are lightly browned and set. Let cool.

Rustic Seed Snacks (Canine "Crackers")

Raw, unsalted seeds and nuts are one of the richest sources of manganese, a nutrient that boosts a dog's humoral immune response and supports a healthy musculoskeletal system. Mix and match your favorite seeds in these manganese-rich cookies.

10 tablespoons raw, unsalted seeds (any combination of chia, whole flax, black or white sesame seeds, hemp hearts, black cumin seeds. If using sunflower or pumpkin seeds, grind to smaller pieces for smaller dogs.)

Pinch of salt

2 teaspoons olive oil

½ cup broth or water (see page 142 for broth ideas)

2 tablespoons almond flour

1. Preheat oven to 250°F.

2. Combine the seeds, salt, and olive oil, add bone broth or water and almond flour, and let set for 10 minutes until the mixture starts to bind together and turns gummy in consistency.

3. Spread mixture to ¼-inch thickness on greased baking sheet, silicone baking mat, or parchment paper.

4. Bake for 1 hour.

5. Carefully turn over cracker with a large spatula and use pizza cutter to cut into desired treat size (½- to 1-inch squares). Continue baking another 30 minutes.

6. Turn off oven and let cracker continue to dry as oven cools down. Remove from oven once cool.

Three-Ingredient Treats

BANANA HONEY TEA BISCUITS

These banana-based biscuits are rich in potassium, with added honey for an antioxidant boost.

Yields 6–8 biscuits

1 medium banana
½ teaspoon raw, local honey
¼ cup almond flour
Optional: sliced almonds for garnish

1. Preheat oven to 250°F.
2. Mash banana in a bowl. Add honey and almond flour; stir to combine thoroughly.
3. Drop by tablespoonful on a greased baking sheet, silicone baking mat, or parchment paper.
4. Top cookies with sliced almonds, if using.
5. Bake for 60 minutes, or until set.

HERBED COTTAGE CRUMPETS

Let your pet get their fill of prebiotic goodness with these cottage cheese–based cookies.

Yields 6–10 cookies

½ cup cottage cheese
2 tablespoons buckwheat flour
1 tablespoon finely chopped fresh herbs
or
1 teaspoon dried herbs of your choice
(rosemary, sage, thyme, parsley, basil, oregano, cilantro, or more—mix and match or use one herb)

1. Preheat oven to 250°F.
2. Mix all ingredients together until well combined.
3. Drop by spoonful onto a greased baking sheet, silicone baking mat, or parchment paper.
4. Bake for 90 minutes.

APPLE CINNAMON TARTS

These tasty tarts are a great source of pectin, the prebiotic fiber in apples that feeds the microbiome. Their cinnamon is also loaded with polyphenols that protect the body from free radical damage and help regulate insulin and blood sugar.

Yields 8–10 tarts

4 ounces (½ cup) unsweetened applesauce
(to make your own applesauce, use the recipe
on page 122)
1 teaspoon ground cinnamon
2 tablespoons coconut flour

1. Preheat oven to 250°F.

2. Mix all ingredients together in a small bowl.

3. Roll dough in small balls (½ to 1 inch, depending on what size treat you want) and place on a greased baking sheet, silicone baking mat, or parchment paper. Flatten slightly with a fork.

4. Bake for 60 minutes or until firm.

COCONUT MACAROONS

This fast-'n'-easy goody stars coconut, which contains antioxidants
that can help protect against DNA damage.

Yields 6–8 cookies, depending on size

1 egg white
1 cup unsweetened shredded coconut
⅓ cup plain kefir

1. Preheat oven to 250°F.

2. Beat the egg white until stiff peaks form.

3. Combine coconut and kefir in a bowl, stirring to combine thoroughly.

4. Gently fold in egg white.

5. Use a cookie scoop or spoon to drop mounds on a greased baking sheet, silicone baking mat, or parchment paper.

6. Bake for 30 minutes or until very lightly browned.

Dr. Holly Ganz's Prebiotic Cookies

One of our favorite microbial ecologists gifted us this recipe, which can also be crumbled into a topper. Sweet potatoes are full of prebiotic fiber but if you purchase them canned, make sure they are unsweetened.

Yields approximately 40 1½-inch cookies

¼ cup whitefish, poached and flaked

¼ cup peanut butter, no sugar or oil

⅔ cup sweet potato puree

1 cup oat flour

¾ cup chickpea flour

1. Preheat oven to 250°F.

2. In a bowl, mix ingredients together.

3. Place on a floured surface. Using a rolling pin, roll into sheets about ¼ to ⅜ inch thick. Cut into desired shapes, rerolling extra dough to make additional cookies.

4. Place cookies on a greased baking sheet, silicone baking mat, or parchment paper. Bake for 2 hours, turning over every 30 minutes until edges are firm and somewhat dry.

Cool Treats

Frozen treats are great to cool off hot dogs or to offer long-lasting enrichment for dogs who like to lick. These recipes can be served many ways, including freeze pops (larger "pupsicles"), thawed and smeared on lick mats, or frozen into silicone molds and tiny treats. Cool treats can also be served as food toppers, in interactive toys as a slushie, or at room temperature (or even warmed, for animals that don't like cold treats). Always supervise animals while enjoying goodies. If you have concerns your dog may try to swallow treats whole, use extra-large molds (like cake or loaf pans) or put frozen treats in a blender for a shaved ice treat. Feed all frozen treats within three months.

Lycopene Lickers

Give your dog this hydrating, immune-bolstering treat on a hot day. Watermelon and tomatoes are loaded with lycopene, a nutrient that stimulates programmed cell death (apoptosis), which means your pup's cellular housecleaning is turned on and amped up. We've also found an occasional cat that shows semi-interest in tasting plain watermelon.

Yields about 24 lickers (using 3 tablespoon molds)

2 cups watermelon, cubed

Optional: ¼ cup kefir or Greek yogurt

2–3 fresh basil leaves (or ½ teaspoon dried)

1. Combine watermelon, kefir or yogurt if using, and basil in blender. Puree until smooth. If your pup prefers a thinner consistency, add filtered water.

2. Freeze in a silicone mold of your choosing.

3. To serve, let thaw slightly in refrigerator until the slush is no longer a solid block of ice.

4. *Optional*: You can make this delectable treat look like a watermelon by creating layers. Freeze pureed watermelon in molds, then add kefir and freeze again. Blend the basil with filtered water, place on top of the watermelon/kefir layers, and freeze again.

Bring on the Basil: Basil is rich in polyphenols and antioxidants, making it anti-inflammatory and anticancer. Adding basil significantly elevates glutathione, catalase, and superoxide dismutase (SOD) levels as well, while also exerting an antidiabetic effect.

Antioxidant Pupsicles

If your dog turns her nose up at greens, this recipe is a great way to sneak them in. It's also a fabulous boredom-buster, as they lick the frozen broth to get to the "prizes" inside.

Fill ice pop molds or paper cups ⅔ full of any combination as follows:

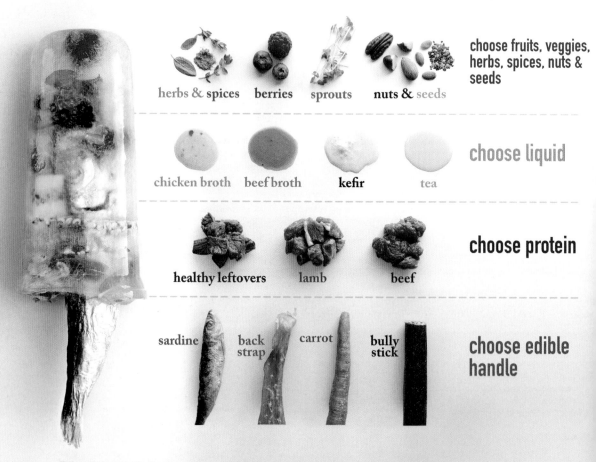

herbs & spices	berries	sprouts	nuts & seeds	**choose fruits, veggies, herbs, spices, nuts & seeds**
chicken broth	beef broth	kefir	tea	**choose liquid**
healthy leftovers	lamb	beef		**choose protein**
sardine	back strap	carrot	bully stick	**choose edible handle**

1.   Fill with broth, kefir, tea, or a combination of all of them.

2.   Add an edible handle if desired (we like fresh asparagus, chicken feet, carrots, or dehydrated tendons).

Leftovers Repurposed: If you don't have ice pop molds for frozen treats, use paper cups instead. Fill the cups with leftovers, freeze them, remove the cup, and watch your pet lick to their heart's content.

Cognition Cubes

This frozen treat mixes brain-friendly coconut oil (rich in MCTs) and cranberries, whose flavonoid content has been shown to improve episodic memory and neural functioning.

Yields 24 cubes (using 3-tablespoon molds)

½ cup coconut oil, room temperature

½ to 1 cup sunflower seed, almond, or nut or seed butter of your choosing

Cranberries, blueberries, or bite-sized fruit of your choosing

1. Coat bottom of ice cube trays or mini muffin molds with coconut oil.

2. Fill mold or tray halfway with seed or nut butter.

3. Add bite-sized fruit on top of the butter.

4. Fill to top with coconut oil and freeze.

Blueberries delay the aging process by facilitating DNA repair.

Adding cranberries to a diet may help improve memory & could protect against dementia.

MCTs in coconut oil have been shown to improve cognition in dogs.

Vitamin E in almond butter keeps cell membranes strong & enhances immune function.

Blue Zone 'Sicles

Sardines are potent sources of vitamin B12—vital for cardiovascular health—and vitamin D, which can help prevent gastrointestinal problems in canines.

Yields ⅔ cup

1 can (3.75 or 4.4 ounces) sardines, packed in water, drained (other options: plain smelt, mussels, oysters, or salmon)

½ cup plain yogurt or kefir

1 teaspoon fresh cilantro, dandelion greens, or sprouts of your choosing, minced

Optional: ⅛ teaspoon rosemary or other herbs of your choice, dried or fresh

1. Puree all ingredients in food processor or blender.

2. To use as a frozen treat: fill silicone molds, toys, or lick mats and freeze.

Longevity Sprout Cubes

Feed this longevity booster as a fun frozen treat, or add to your pet's bowl, coat with liquid, and watch it melt into a topper.

5 ounces sprouts of your choosing, raw

⅔ cup filtered water or broth

1. Puree sprouts and liquid in a blender or food processor.

2. Pour sprouts mixture into ice cube trays.

3. Freeze and store for up to 3 months.

Feed one ice cube per thirty pounds of body weight per day.

A Word on Broth: See page 142 for a full discussion of broths, but if you choose to buy a commercial broth (for example, to use in this recipe), always pick one that's free of onions and low in sodium.

Dandelion Gut Cubes

Dandelion greens are fiber-rich gems that stimulate bile in the liver, which then filters out toxins into the feces. Freeze these and use them as a tasty, nutritious topper.

5 ounces fresh dandelion greens

⅔ cup filtered water or broth

1. Chop greens, place in ice cube trays, and cover with water, or puree greens and water in a blender or food processor.

2. Pour greens mixture into ice cube trays and freeze.

Feed one ice cube per thirty pounds of body weight per day.

Save Your Dandelion Flowers: While this recipe calls for the greens, don't toss out the dandelion flowers. In dandelions, polyphenols are concentrated 115 times more in the flowers than in the roots. Rinse and dry them thoroughly (to prevent fungal growth), then blend and add them to ice cubes, chop and mix them with your pet's food, or dehydrate them to create dandelion powder.

Toppers with a Purpose

Toppers with a Purpose allow you to supercharge your pet's food right at mealtime. Each tailored for a different condition or concern, they offer longevity-boosting benefits that enhance pets' microbiomes, support their immune systems, rebuild their cells, and more. Unless we indicate otherwise, you can add whatever topper you choose to your pet's food, spread it on a lick mat or in a toy, or freeze for future fun.

Store all toppers in the refrigerator for three days or freezer for three months (unless noted otherwise).

Suggested Serving Size: A dollop (1–2 tablespoons) per twenty pounds of body weight per day. Always start with smaller amounts until your animal adjusts to new flavors.

Expand Your Enrichment Opportunities: Dogs often have *hours* of absolutely nothing every day, so enrichment is crucial for their health. Food is enrichment all on its own, but let's not miss the opportunity to take it a step further: if your dog has to solve a puzzle, conduct a search, or even lick through a frosty (but nutritious) layer to devour the tasty treasure hidden inside, his body and brain win. Plus, channeling his energy and curiosity into enrichment activities means he will be less likely to resort to devising his own (like chewing on the furniture).

Choline Cognition Topper

If this recipe yields large chunks, use them as training treats. Otherwise, grind and sprinkle "crumbs" on food or a lick mat for a choline-filled topper or enrichment activity.

9 eggs yield 1 cup powder

Eggs (as many as you choose), shelled

Optional: coconut or avocado oil, as needed

1. Preheat oven to 170°F.

2. Whisk eggs until thoroughly combined in a bowl.

3. Coat a pan with a very thin layer of coconut or avocado oil (if needed).

4. Pour egg mixture into pan and cook over low heat, gently stirring and folding eggs until fully cooked.

5. Remove from pan and place on parchment paper–covered baking sheet.

6. Place in oven and cook 4–6 hours, or until completely dry.

Cranberry Sardine Chutney

Cranberries bolster bladder and brain health, but they're tart, so we like cooking them in a savory broth or in leftover sardine water.

Yields 4 ounces

1 3.75-ounce can sardines, packed in water

⅓ cup fresh cranberries

⅛ cup water, broth of your choice, or retained sardine water

½ teaspoon gelatin powder

Optional: 1 tablespoon kefir

1. Drain sardines, reserving ⅛ cup liquid to chill (and additional ⅛ cup if desired to cook cranberries).

2. Combine the cranberries and ⅛ cup broth, water, or sardine water in a small saucepan.

3. Simmer over low heat until the cranberries become soft enough to smash with a fork, about 5–10 minutes. Remove from heat.

4. Stir in gelatin powder.

5. Stir in chilled ⅛ cup water, broth, or sardine water.

6. Add sardines and mash together or combine in a food processor.

7. Add kefir if desired.

Pinches of Prebiotics

This egg roll–inspired prebiotic topper packs in cabbage, one of the most nutritionally dense vegetables in the world (full of vitamins C and K, potassium, prebiotic fiber, protein, and the antioxidant anthocyanin, which fights inflammation and lowers the risk of cardiovascular disease).

¼ cup carrot, small diced or shredded

½ cup mushrooms, diced

½ teaspoon ginger, finely grated

1 cup green cabbage, shredded

For cooked version: 1 teaspoon coconut oil

1. Mix all ingredients in a large bowl and serve raw as a meal topper, on a lick mat, or in an interactive toy.

2. Or, to cook, heat 1 teaspoon coconut oil in a large fry pan over medium-low heat.

3. Add the carrot and sauté for a few minutes.

4. Add the mushrooms and cook until they begin to soften.

5. Add the ginger and stir to combine.

6. Add the cabbage, mixing in thoroughly.

7. Cover and let cook for 3–5 minutes, until cabbage has wilted and softened slightly.

Serve freshly shredded
or cooked

Tabouli Biome Topper

In this topper, it's out with the bad (gut bacteria), in with the good (gut bacteria). Parsley is rich in a substance called apigenin, a dietary flavonoid that stimulates the growth of certain good gut bacteria, and the menthol in peppermint can mitigate the damage from bad bacteria, including *H. pylori* and *E. coli*.

1 tablespoon fresh parsley, chopped

1 tablespoon fresh mint, chopped

½ cup tomato, diced

1 cup cucumber, diced

In a small bowl, combine all ingredients.

Start with ¼ cup per twenty pounds of body weight.

Pad Thai Topper

This Thai-inspired topper holds one of the secret ingredients to longevity: resveratrol, a potent antioxidant that protects against cell damage.

½ cup sprouts of your choosing or
1 tablespoon sprouted peanuts
(see page 66)

1 teaspoon fresh cilantro, chopped,
or ½ teaspoon dried

1 egg, poached

Optional: lime squeeze as garnish

1. Sprinkle the sprouts or sprouted peanuts (chop for small dogs) and cilantro over your dog's meal, then place poached egg on top.

2. If desired, squeeze the lime over top to boost vitamin C. Mix well.

This topper is about eighty calories per serving, a respectable-sized topper for dogs over fifty pounds. Medium-sized dogs can enjoy half the recipe once a day or several times a week. One batch can easily become four servings for small dogs and cats.

Prioritize Peanut Sprouts: Pets just love peanut sprouts for their sweet and buttery flavor, and pet parents love them because they are a rich source of polyphenols, including resveratrol, the powerful antioxidant most famous for giving red wine its color. Resveratrol is anti-inflammatory, anticancer, boosts heart health, aids in improving alertness and cognitive function, and reduces the risk for dementia. Sprouted peanuts contain ninety times the amount of resveratrol of wine!

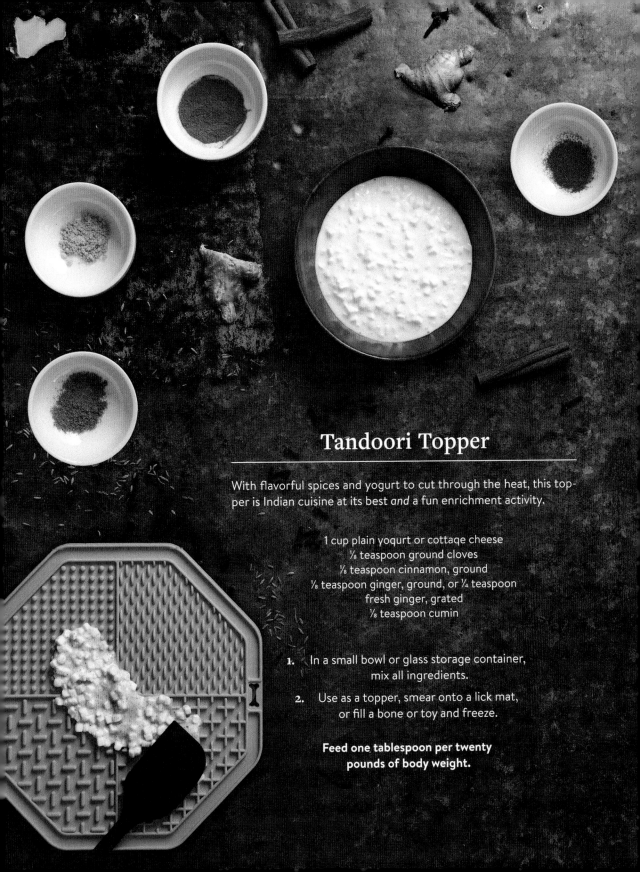

Tandoori Topper

With flavorful spices and yogurt to cut through the heat, this topper is Indian cuisine at its best *and* a fun enrichment activity.

1 cup plain yogurt or cottage cheese
⅛ teaspoon ground cloves
⅛ teaspoon cinnamon, ground
⅛ teaspoon ginger, ground, or ¼ teaspoon fresh ginger, grated
⅛ teaspoon cumin

1. In a small bowl or glass storage container, mix all ingredients.

2. Use as a topper, smear onto a lick mat, or fill a bone or toy and freeze.

Feed one tablespoon per twenty pounds of body weight.

Fiber Smoothie

This recipe's fiber-rich apples and pineapples (which also contain the enzyme bromelain) aid digestion, bulk up stools, and provide anal gland support to pets in need.

½ cup plain, unsweetened organic yogurt

½ cup unsweetened 100 percent pure pineapple juice
(if your dog is picky, use broth—see page 142)

1 tablespoon psyllium husk powder

1 small apple, with skin, cored, seeded,
and chopped

Puree all ingredients in a blender or food processor.

Apples=Anal Gland Rescue: Your animal's anal glands are located on either side of his anus, and they release a small amount of liquid every time he poops (providing a download of personal biologic pheromone data, if you're a fellow dog). If they're enlarged, impacted, or inflamed, apples—which are a rich source of pectin (a soluble fiber)—paired with the bulking power of psyllium husk and a dose of bromelain (the anti-inflammatory proteolytic enzyme found in pineapple) provide the perfect blend of ingredients for healthy anal gland expression. Plus, *even a single dose* of a type of polyphenol in apples, called B-type procyanidins, can activate the gut-brain axis, which helps to improve cognitive function and reduce the risk of cognitive decline.

Make Your Own Applesauce

It's sweet and savory, made with bone broth instead of water.

6 apples, cored and chopped

¼ cup bone broth

1. Place ingredients in small saucepan.
2. Simmer on low heat for 30 minutes, or until apples are soft enough to easily mash with a fork. If needed, add more broth or apples to reach desired consistency.
3. Let cool and smear on a lick mat, use as a topper, or use in a recipe.
4. Store remaining applesauce in the refrigerator for up to a week.

Smart Spread

With fermented food and omega-rich seafood, this spreadable topper is good for the gut and the brain.

1 cup cooked salmon
(fresh or canned and packed in water, drained)
or other "clean" seafood (see page 56)

½ cup plain yogurt

½ cup cooked mushrooms (see page 47)
or ¼ cup sprouts (see page 66)

4 tablespoons raw pumpkin seeds

Optional: 1–3 teaspoons DIY Vitamin/Mineral Greens Powder
(see page 127)

In a blender or food processor, puree ingredients.

Offer one ounce as a topper or on a lick mat per ten pounds of body weight per day. Or freeze in an ice cube tray or silicone mold for future use.

Try Kefir: Don't let yogurt be the only fermented food you feed your pet. Kefir is yogurt's runnier, tangier, and sourer cousin, and it contains up to one thousand times more beneficial bacteria than yogurt. Research shows dogs who are fed kefir have a healthier gut within two weeks! Add one tablespoon of kefir per ten pounds of body weight per day to your dog's food.

Enrichment Extends Lives: Chronic stress can cause a host of health problems, from gastrointestinal illnesses to immune dysfunction to depression to cardiovascular disease. Providing enriching activities—like walking, playing with other animals, or offering lick mats, toys, or a food-dispensing toy full of healthy tidbits and toppers—can help combat stress-related behaviors such as anxiety, depression, marking, aggression, and antisocial behavior.

Don't have a snuffle mat? Use a head of leafy lettuce! Tucking a variety of small, healthy morsels between the leaves gives your dog (or cat) an opportunity to exercise her nose and brain as she finds each hidden prize.

It's up to you to make wise decisions for your pet, however. If you know your puppy will attempt to chew and swallow pieces of a DIY enrichment opportunity (like an eggshell carton), don't set them up for failure (or injury). Only offer food formats and food-dispensing devices that you know your animal can enjoy safely, and in portions that make sense for your animal (you can always limit enrichment sessions to a few minutes, putting leftovers back in the fridge for another session later). Always supervise your pets while they're enjoying food, treats, and toys so you can intervene if needed.

Slow down mealtime gobblers by dishing up dinner in a muffin tin, or offer a buffet of healthy treats or toppers in each well to nourish your dog's body and mind.

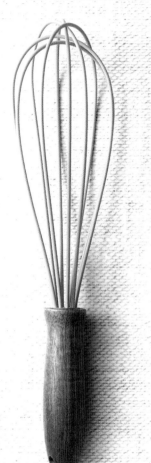

Shrimp Whip

Shrimp is a great source of iodine, and it also contains a neuroprotective antioxidant that gives shrimp its pink color: astaxanthin.

Yields approximately ⅔ cup

½ teaspoon gelatin

¼ cup broth, hot

½ cup cooked shrimp, minced fine (or canned)

1. Place the gelatin in a bowl.

2. Pour the hot broth over the gelatin and whisk to mix thoroughly.

3. Fold in the minced shrimp until fully combined.

4. Mixture will thicken as it cools. Whisk or puree when cool, prior to serving.

liquid of choice

turmeric powder

Whisk to mix thoroughly

The Ultimate 2.0 Turmeric Paste

This paste is rich in brain-boosting turmeric. Turmeric's primary compound is curcumin, which has been found to increase levels of brain-derived neurotrophic factor (BDNF), a protein that supports the healthy function of neurons.

Yields approximately 1½ cups

½ cup turmeric powder

1–2 cups filtered water, mushroom broth (see recipe on page 146), or decaffeinated tea (see suggestions on page 149) for desired consistency

¼–⅓ cup coconut oil (or lard, grass-fed butter, avocado oil, or MCT oil)

½ teaspoon freshly ground black pepper OR ground ginger

¼ cup mushroom powder

1. Add turmeric and water, broth, or tea to a small pot.

2. Whisk to mix thoroughly.

3. Simmer over low to medium heat for 7–10 minutes, whisking until paste forms.

4. Turn off heat and add oil.

5. Add black pepper and mushroom powder. Whisk well.

Start with ¼ teaspoon and work up to ¼ teaspoon per ten pounds of body weight.

grass-fed butter

mct oil

coconut oil

avocado oil

lard

ground ginger

or

black pepper

mushroom powder

Apoptosis Add-Ins
(Curcumin Cream Cheese)

This creamy topper is powerful magic for your pet's brain, cells, *and* blood sugar. Apoptosis is natural, programmed cell death—often used by the body to prevent cancerous cell growth—and curcumin has been found to induce it. Even more than turmeric, curcumin alone can also lower diabetes markers. Because its powder comes in different strengths, we've recommended a dose that will provide general health benefits but should not be used as treatment for specific health conditions.

Yields approximately ½ cup

4 ounces cream cheese

1 teaspoon curcumin powder

1 teaspoon mushroom powder

¼ teaspoon ground ginger or freshly ground black pepper

Mix all ingredients until well combined.

Offer one teaspoon per ten pounds of body weight, mixed in food or on a lick mat, per day.

DIY Vitamin/Mineral Greens Powder

Sometimes what's good for your pet is also good for your wallet. You can spend up to $100 on a container of powdered greens—or you can make your own following this recipe. This DIY super greens powder is a great way to use up greens and sneak more superfoods into your pet's diet.

Yields approximately 4 tablespoons

4½ cups of greens (kale, spinach, or dandelion greens of your choice)

1. Preheat oven to its lowest setting.

2. Wash and dry greens thoroughly. Remove stems from kale leaves and chop or rip leaves to a similar size. You can leave spinach as is.

3. Lay flat on a greased baking sheet, silicone baking mat, or parchment paper and cook for 6–8 hours or until completely dry and crispy. Or place on racks in a dehydrator for 6–8 hours at 125°F.

4. Blend or grind dried greens until they reach a powder consistency.

5. Store in an airtight container in a cool, dark place (we like the fridge). Use powder within a month.

Add to meals or dust over a lick mat that's been smeared with shrimp whip (see page 124), cottage cheese, or mashed sardines. Use ½ teaspoon for every ten pounds of body weight.

DIY Lion's Mane Mushroom Powder

Rodney's dog, Shubie, hates mushrooms, so this recipe is one of Rodney's favorite ways to sneak a healthy dose of good-for-the-gut medicinal mushrooms into her food.

Yields approximately ⅔ cup

4½ cups lion's mane mushrooms

1. Preheat oven to 170°F.

2. Wash and dry mushrooms thoroughly.

3. Slice or pull apart into ⅛-inch pieces.

4. Place in a single layer on a greased baking sheet, silicone baking mat, or parchment paper.

5. Prop open the oven door with a wooden spoon and bake 5 hours, turning mushrooms over midway through the cooking time. Or, in a dehydrator, place in a single layer on racks and dehydrate for 6 to 8 hours at 125°F or until completely dried and crispy. If you live in a drier climate, you can also leave uncovered indoors and let dry about six days or until completely dried and crispy.

6. Pulse in a blender or food processor to make powder.

7. Store in an airtight container in a dry, cool place (refrigerator works well). Use up in a month.

Feed ½ teaspoon per ten pounds of body weight, dusted on food, mixed in a topper, or dusted over a lick mat, per day.

Lion's Mane Is Good for the Gut: Study after study shows that this medicinal mushroom stimulates the production of nerve cells, helps neurons regenerate, and reduces oxidative stress. But these miraculous mushrooms are even *better* than we originally thought. Elderly dogs fed lion's mane mushroom show a significantly better balance of beneficial gut bacteria as compared to harmful bacteria, demonstrating clearly that they can help regulate the gut microbial community.

Gelatin, Gravies, Jellies, and Jigglers

Gelatin is the star in this section's recipes, so it's time to think of it as something more than an ingredient in a sugary dessert. In fact, it's a versatile thickener (the more gelatin you add, the firmer your creation will be) and benefits the joints, hair, skin, and more.

Gelatin is nature's richest source of the amino acid glycine, which detoxifies environmental pollutants like glyphosate. It also makes mammals feel full, so it's a satisfying and nutritious ingredient for all sorts of DIY treats. Gelatin is *great* for the gut, strengthening the lining of the digestive system by protecting its gastric mucus. Gelatin also improves the secretion of certain stomach acids, which aids digestion, and absorbs water, which keeps fluid and waste products moving along through the digestive tract. Gelatin also supports cartilage health, can reduce joint pain, and even helps with hair growth!

You can find plain gelatin powder in your grocery store, though we prefer grass-fed, pasture-raised beef gelatin from health food stores or online. Unless we indicate otherwise, store your gelatin, gravies, jellies, and jigglers in a sealed container in the refrigerator for three days or the freezer for up to three months. Slice gelatin treats into sizes your pet can safely consume.

One tablespoon of plain gelatin (about seven grams) contains approximately twenty-four calories and is fat-free, making it awesome for everyone. Match the gelatin consistency and add-ins to what's best for your beast.

How to Make the Perfect Gelatin Consistency

You can customize the density of gelatin treats by adjusting the amount of gelatin. If you have a dog who needs a softer bone, use less. The more gelatin you add, the firmer the treat will be.

Gelatin Gravy

Terrific as a topper

Yields ½ cup

½ teaspoon gelatin in
½ cup broth or tea (see pages 142 and 149)

Gelatin Tennis Ball

An extra-squishy reward

Yields one ball

4 tablespoons gelatin in
1 cup broth or tea

Use silicone ball ice cube molds
or metal "bath bomb" molds.

Gelatin Jelly

Great for a food topper or lick mat

Yields ½ cup

1 rounded teaspoon gelatin in
½ cup broth or tea

Gelatin Frisbee

A firm treat that's great for enrichment
Use a pie dish to create the Frisbee shape.

Yields one Frisbee

6–8 tablespoons gelatin in
1 cup broth or tea

Gelatin Jiggler

Makes an excellent pill pouch

Yield depends on size of mold

1 tablespoon gelatin in
½ cup broth or tea

Gelatin Bones (extra firm)

Gel-O Bones can provide extended enrichment for professional lickers. Stuff them—as on page 130—with complete and balanced food, toppers, or peanut butter. You can also top them with whatever your dog desires—as shown below—then freeze them to make soothing and satisfying teething toys for puppies or a refreshing summertime treat.

Yield depends on size of bone molds

8–12 tablespoons (½–¾ cup) gelatin in 1 cup broth or tea (depending on how hard you want the bone to be)

1. For all gelatin: mix broth or tea and gelatin until dissolved. Let sit until mixture thickens to a jelly consistency. Pour into greased mold or storage container (we like coconut or avocado oil) and refrigerate for 3 hours. If the mold doesn't have a bottom (like a cookie cutter), press it firmly while filling. Add chopped tidbits or toppers, if desired.

2. For harder bones that use more gelatin, the mixture will be very thick. We use a whisk to mix. Moisten fingers and press mixture into mold.

3. Refrigerate extras for up to a week or freeze for later use. Thaw before feeding.

4. Always supervise while enjoying. Do not offer to dogs that try to swallow everything whole, or chop into bite-sized pieces prior to feeding, treating, or training.

Gelatin Can Vary: Gelatin consistency can depend on the brand, whether you choose plain, multipurpose gelatin or beef gelatin powder, and what kind of liquid (water, tea, broth) you use to make it. Some gelatin brands also require you to use room temperature liquid, while others call for hot. Finally, some gelatin may harden faster than others—or when smaller quantities of powder are used. Check labels, experiment with the brand you choose, start with a small amount, and increase as needed.

Gut Gummies

Gelatin powder (See gelatin ratio recipes on page 131 for desired consistency. Double the amount of gelatin if using fresh ginger.)

1 tablespoon slippery elm powder or marshmallow root powder

½ teaspoon dried ginger (or 1 teaspoon fresh ginger)

Optional: 1 tablespoon activated charcoal powder (excellent for pets with diarrhea)

Optional: 1 probiotic capsule or ⅛ cup plain kefir

2 cups hot broth or tea of your choice (see page 149 for more on tea)

Optional: 1 teaspoon Manuka honey or royal jelly

Optional: 1 tablespoon inner leaf aloe juice

1. Combine all dry ingredients (except probiotic capsule) in a large bowl.

2. Carefully whisk in hot broth or tea to dissolve all powders. Decrease the amount of liquid you use by equal amount of optional liquids used (kefir, honey, jelly, aloe juice).

3. Let cool and add probiotics (removing the capsule), honey, jelly, juice, kefir, if using. Stir to fully combine.

4. Refrigerate 3 hours to allow the gelatin to set.

Gelatin versus Collagen: Collagen and gelatin have similar chemical structures, but they differ in their properties and uses. Collagen is an abundant, naturally occurring protein that provides structural support for skin, bones, cartilage, and tendons. Gelatin is derived from collagen by a process that breaks down the long collagen fibers into shorter, more soluble protein molecules, resulting in a gel-like substance.

Edible Tennis Balls

For the ultimate enrichment game, toss an edible tennis ball filled with dog-friendly foods from the fridge. When playtime is over, your dog can eat his way to the healthy goodies suspended inside.

Yields one 1-cup ball or two ½-cup balls

Coconut or avocado oil

½ cup diced add-ins of choice: fruits, vegetables, meats, fish, or more, if desired (you can also make plain broth or tea balls)

4 tablespoons gelatin powder

1 cup broth or tea

1. Lightly grease both halves of a ball mold with coconut or avocado oil.

2. Place ¼ cup of the add-ins in each half of the mold.

3. In separate bowl, sprinkle gelatin powder over broth or tea and stir to dissolve. Let sit until it starts to thicken.

4. Pour liquid-gelatin mixture into each ball mold half, filling to rim.

5. Let sit until the mixture becomes the consistency of thick jelly, and won't run out of molds, then press one ball half on top of the other. Wipe away the excess.

6. Refrigerate 3 hours or until firm.

7. Gently remove ball from mold.

Mix-and-Match Molds

The options for gelatin are truly limitless. While we purchased metal "bath bomb" molds and silicone ice cube ball molds online to make our "edible tennis ball" shape, you can customize your gelatin creation to the kitchenware you have on hand and your dog's needs.

Choose any clean vessel that holds liquids (we've used mini loaf pans, coffee mugs, small serving bowls, and muffin tins to make gelatin treats). Just make sure it fits in your fridge. You can add in new foods you want to highlight or introduce, from berries and raw seeds or nuts you need to use up, to vegetable trimmings and last night's healthy dinner leftovers. Dice add-ins to an appropriate size for your pup. Plain broth, with a pinch of sea salt, works just fine, too.

Here, we use the same ratios as in the tennis balls. Feel free to size these ingredients up or down, depending on the size of the mold you are filling. Also note that some add-ins may require additional gelatin to solidify. If your concoction is too jiggly, try doubling the gelatin next time—and spread the jelly on a lick mat!

Coconut or avocado oil

¼–½ cup veggie, fruit, or meat add-ins
(can also use broth or tea alone)

4 tablespoons gelatin powder makes extra-firm treats; use 3 tablespoons for softer, more jiggly texture

1 cup broth or tea
(see pages 139–151 for inspiration)

Optional: 1 tablespoon plain yogurt or kefir

1. Lightly oil your mold with coconut or avocado oil.

2. Place your add-ins in the mold.

3. In a separate bowl, sprinkle the gelatin powder over the broth or tea (plus optional yogurt or kefir, if desired) and stir to dissolve (will form a jelly-like consistency).

4. Pour the gelatin mixture over the fruit/veggie/meat add-ins in the mold.

5. If using cookie cutter–type molds, line a baking tray with parchment paper and press firmly on mold while filling. Refrigerate for 4 hours, or until set. Remove from mold and serve (with supervision).

How to Unstick Gelatin: If you struggle to get your gelatin creation out of a mold, try soaking it in hot water. That will help release the sticky gelatin from the sides.

Forever Fluids

What do humans eat when they're sick or seeking comfort? Chicken soup, tea, smoothies, and nutrient-dense juices. Fluids heal and hydrate, and pets need them as much as we do. These Forever Fluids are concentrated medicinal infusions, packed with nutrients and compounds that are easily absorbed, which increases their bioavailability. They're also inexpensive ways to supercharge your pets' meals with longevity-boosting ingredients.

Feed your pet one to two ounces (two to four tablespoons for every ten pounds of body weight) to start. Big batches or leftovers can be stored in the refrigerator for up to five days or the freezer for three months (if you choose, you can portion into ice cube trays).

option 1

Serve this as a
chunky soup.

Root Vegetable Super Stew

This nutrient-dense super stew contains turnips, whose compound sulforaphane activates genes responsible for fighting inflammation. Sulforaphanes also slow the rate of cancer and cardiovascular biomarkers, reduce inflammation, and remove toxins from the body.

Serve this as a chunky soup or puree it into a topper.

Yields 6–8 cups

1 medium turnip, peeled and diced into ½- to 1-inch cubes

1 medium parsnip, peeled and diced into ½- to 1-inch cubes

1 small rutabaga, peeled and diced into ½- to 1-inch cubes

2–3 Jerusalem artichokes, diced into ½- to 1-inch cubes

1 daikon, peeled and diced into ½- to 1-inch cubes

1 medium or 6–8 baby carrots, sliced into ½-inch coins

1 large beet, peeled and diced into ½- to 1-inch cubes

1 small sweet potato, diced into ½- to 1-inch cubes

4–8 cups broth (bone, chicken, beef, mushroom, etc.),
or as much as needed to cover vegetables

Optional: herbal tea bag
(see page 149 for inspirations), 2 teaspoons fresh
or 1 teaspoon dried herbs (see page 70), added while cooling

1. Place all vegetables in large soup pot, then pour in 4 cups broth. Add more broth if vegetables are not covered.

2. Bring to a boil, then lower heat and simmer 30 minutes or until veggies are tender.

3. Add 1–2 tea bags of choice while stew cools, along with fresh or dried herbs.

4. Remove tea bags when broth is cool. Puree to smooth consistency if desired.

5. *Slow cooker method*: Place vegetables and broth in Crock-Pot, cook on low for 8 hours, then add tea and herbs once heat is turned off. Remove tea bags when broth is cool.

option 2

Puree it into
a topper.

Best Bone Broth

Bone broth is good health in a pot, providing collagen for joint support and gut health. Served warm as a topper or on its own like a soup, bone broth is comforting, healing, and always delicious.

Yields approximately 8 cups

3 pounds any bones
(chicken, marrow, knuckle/joint bones, etc.)

8–10 cups filtered water

2 tablespoons apple cider vinegar

Optional for joint support: decaf green tea
or turmeric

Optional: piece of raw backstrap or joint bones
(these contain more collagen, so they create extra-gooey,
gelatinous broth, especially beef tendon)

Optional: chicken or duck feet (these are also rich
in collagen and will create a gelatinous broth)

1. Place bones in slow cooker. Add backstrap or feet if using. Add enough filtered water to just cover contents by ½ to 1 inch. Add apple cider vinegar.

2. Cook on medium-high heat for one hour then reduce to low. Keep a very gentle boil where the surface of the liquid is moving with only occasional small bubbles appearing. (If cooking low and slow, there should be minimal evaporation. If liquid is evaporating, add more water and decrease cooking temperature.)

3. Let cool, discard bones, and strain through fine mesh strainer into clean glass containers (to remove small, splintered bones).

4. Skim and discard fat before freezing or serving.

Slow cooker cooking times:
- **Chicken bones:** 24 hours
- **Dense bones (beef, bison, lamb):** 48 hours

Bone Broth Heals: Bone broth builds up the immune system and helps fight ulcerative colitis by decreasing the expression of pro-inflammatory cytokines (proteins that control immune and blood cell growth) and stimulating the expression of anti-inflammatory cytokines in animal models.

Building Broths for Health

There are endless variations of delicious and nutritious broths you can create, so we've made it easy here by providing three recipes that treat common conditions your pet may experience. The steps to build each are the same, though the ingredients differ.

Yields 6–10 cups

Steps to Build Your Broth

1. Choose a recipe.

2. Finely chop veggies and herbs.

3. Add all ingredients to a stockpot filled with 3 quarts filtered water.

4. Cover and simmer on low heat, just below boiling, for 1 hour, stirring occasionally.

5. Turn off heat and add tea bags, if desired. Let cool. Skim off fat if you want low-fat broth.

6. Remove any tea bags and bones and strain and compost or discard solids. Pour liquid into glass storage container and store, refrigerated, for up to 5 days, or freeze for up to 3 months for later use (1-ounce ice cube trays work well).

7. Thaw and use to reconstitute freeze-dried or dehydrated pet food, add to dry food as a topper, freeze on a lick mat, or substitute for any recipe that calls for water.

Belly-Soothing Broth

1 pound fresh or leftover poultry, lamb or venison bones, or beef knuckle bone (in most grocery stores labeled as "soup bones")

½ fennel bulb
(prevents GI ulcers)

2-inch piece of ginger root
(reduces acid reflux and nausea, improves GI motility)

2-inch piece of turmeric root
(anti-inflammatory)

1 cup dandelion greens or Jerusalem artichokes
(source of inulin)

1 teaspoon ground cumin
(increases digestive enzyme activity and eases gas)

Optional: finely chopped fresh or dried herbs of your choosing (if you don't have fresh herbs, you can swap for two tea bags containing the same herbs):

1 teaspoon lemon balm
(regulates motility and reduces gas)

1 teaspoon peppermint
(soothes indigestion)

1 teaspoon chamomile
(antispasmodic)

To cook, follow steps above.

Brain-Building Broth

1 cup ground fresh salmon (reduces risk of neurological inflammation)

1 tablespoon rosemary (protects against cognitive decline)

1 tablespoon sage (neuroprotective)

1 cinnamon stick or 1 teaspoon ground cinnamon (improves cognitive performance)

To cook, follow steps above.

1 teaspoon oregano
(enhances feeling of mental well-being)

Optional: finely chopped fresh or dried herbs of your choosing (if you don't have fresh herbs, you can swap for two tea bags containing the same herbs):

Pinch of saffron (protects the brain from neurotoxins)

Pinch of finely ground black pepper (slows neurodegeneration)

Two decaf green tea bags (protects against oxidation)

Immune Broth

1 beef marrow bone
(or 3 pieces of oxtail from grocery store)

1 cup reishi mushrooms
(regulates the immune system)

1 tablespoon cilantro
(antimicrobial, anti-inflammatory)

1 tablespoon curly parsley
(assists in detoxification)

To cook, follow steps above.

1 tablespoon oregano
(antifungal benefits)

2 cloves fresh garlic
(antimicrobial, immune-modulating)

Optional: finely chopped fresh or dried herbs of your choosing (if you don't have fresh herbs, you can swap for two tea bags containing the same herbs):

2x2-inch piece of chaga mushroom

2 tablespoons manuka honey (stir in *after* broth is done simmering and removed from heat)

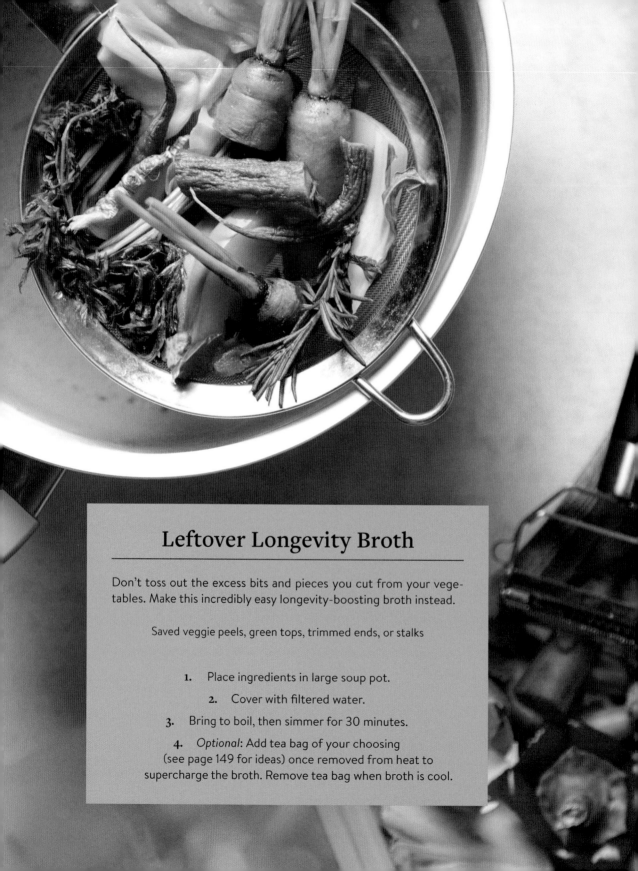

Leftover Longevity Broth

Don't toss out the excess bits and pieces you cut from your vegetables. Make this incredibly easy longevity-boosting broth instead.

Saved veggie peels, green tops, trimmed ends, or stalks

1. Place ingredients in large soup pot.
2. Cover with filtered water.
3. Bring to boil, then simmer for 30 minutes.
4. *Optional*: Add tea bag of your choosing (see page 149 for ideas) once removed from heat to supercharge the broth. Remove tea bag when broth is cool.

Quick and Easy Low-Histamine Bone Broth

Histamine is a compound naturally produced by immune cells in response to an allergic trigger, and if your dog is itchy, irritated, or scratching at their goopy eyes, they're probably full of it. Bones are full of it, too, and the longer you cook them, the more histamine is released from the marrow. We cook our bone broth for only a few hours to keep the levels low, in case your dog might be histamine-intolerant.

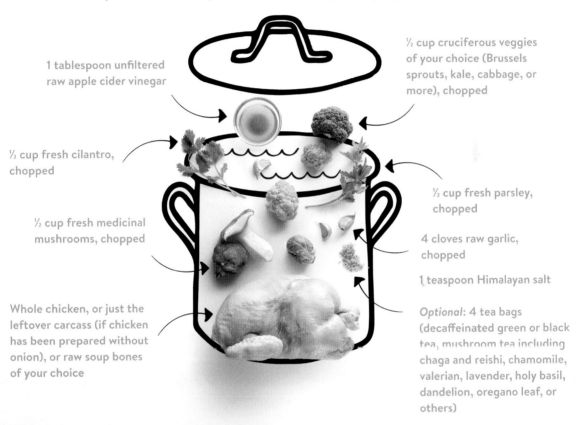

1 tablespoon unfiltered raw apple cider vinegar

½ cup cruciferous veggies of your choice (Brussels sprouts, kale, cabbage, or more), chopped

½ cup fresh cilantro, chopped

½ cup fresh medicinal mushrooms, chopped

½ cup fresh parsley, chopped

4 cloves raw garlic, chopped

1 teaspoon Himalayan salt

Whole chicken, or just the leftover carcass (if chicken has been prepared without onion), or raw soup bones of your choice

Optional: 4 tea bags (decaffeinated green or black tea, mushroom tea including chaga and reishi, chamomile, valerian, lavender, holy basil, dandelion, oregano leaf, or others)

1. Place the chicken/carcass in a large pot and add enough pure filtered water to completely cover. Add the rest of the ingredients.

2. Cover the pot and simmer over low heat for 4 hours.

3. Turn off the heat and add 4 tea bags if desired.

4. Steep the tea bags for 10 minutes, then remove the bags from the pot.

5. Discard bones, first removing any remaining meat (put the meat back in the broth).

6. Puree the meat, veggies, and broth to a gravy-like consistency using an immersion blender. A regular blender will also work, but process in batches to fit the blender, once the broth is cool enough to safely handle.

7. Freeze the broth in individual portions, such as in ice cube trays or silicone molds.

Super-Immune Mushroom Broth

Full of immune-boosting beta-glucans, mushroom broth is liquid gold for the immune system. We like using ground turmeric and ginger in this recipe, but add any spices you choose—or none at all.

2 cups medicinal mushrooms, sliced

1 tablespoon unsalted butter

6 cups filtered water, broth, or herbal tea

Optional: 1 tablespoon herbs or spices
(choose based on your pet's health and conditions
—see page 70)

1. Sauté mushrooms in butter over low heat until soft.

2. Add filtered water, broth, or tea.

3. Add herbs or spices, if desired.

4. Simmer for 3–5 minutes.

5. Let cool until able to handle.

6. Puree using an immersion blender, or in a blender (in batches if necessary).

7. May be served warm or cool.

Spotlight on Shiitakes: While you can use any type of mushroom in this recipe, we love shiitakes! This magnificent mushroom contains a carbohydrate called lentinan that can effectively treat gastric cancer, and, in fact, it's been approved for use as treatment for gastric cancer patients in Japan. Lentinan also reduces the cell damage done by the environmental toxin benzy(a)pyrene (found in car exhaust, smoke, and other burning fuels), which can cause skin, bladder, and lung cancer in humans and animals.

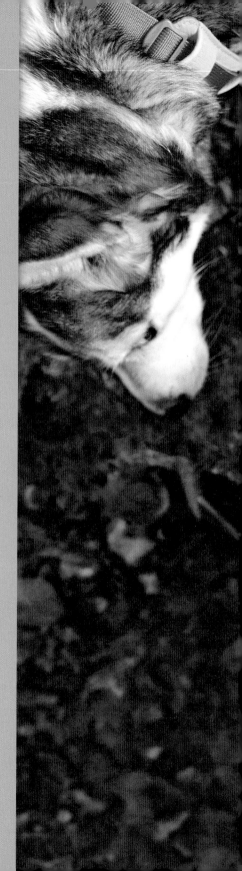

Gingermeric Gravy

This super-fragrant gravy is brain-boosting, gut-soothing, and—because it contains cinnamon—heart-healthy. Most of us don't think about feeding our dogs cinnamon, but studies show that dogs given cinnamon see improved heart performance and blood pressure—key measures of heart health.

1 teaspoon turmeric root powder

½ teaspoon ginger

1 tablespoon coconut or olive oil

Dash ground cinnamon

⅓ cup hot filtered water, hot broth, or tea

1. Mix first four ingredients in a bowl or cup.
2. Add hot liquid to mixture, stir, and let cool.

Serving Suggestion: Add a tablespoon per twenty pounds of body weight to food once a day or split between daily feedings.

Teas, Straight Up

In theory, animals have been consuming tea for millennia; every time a leaf falls off a plant or tree and lands in a puddle of water, the outcome is essentially tea. Cooled teas are an economical and powerful way to deliver a plant's best medicinal properties directly to your dog or cat. Teas make inexpensive, polyphenol-rich toppers ("gravies") that infuse antioxidants and bioactive plant chemicals into every meal.

Types of Teas

- **Decaf green and black tea:** Loaded with bioactive compounds that have powerful anti-inflammatory, antioxidant, and pro-immune effects. Green tea has long been documented to improve brain function, protect against cancer, and lower risk of heart disease. Both green and black tea are a rich source of theaflavins, a group of antioxidant molecules that are created from catechins, and both contain the calming amino acid L-theanine, which alleviates stress in the body.

- **Herbal tea:** Made from a variety of different herbs, these brews are all naturally decaffeinated and can benefit the body and mind in many ways, depending on the medicinal properties of the herb. In addition to popular teas you can find at your local health food store, including rooibos (African red tea), rose hip, passionflower, and valerian ("sleepy time") teas, pets can also enjoy fresh herbal infusions from your garden, including catnip, peppermint, hibiscus, sage, echinacea, lemon verbena, lemon balm, lemongrass, linden flower, calendula, basil, and fennel.

Bring 8 ounces of filtered water to a near boil and add teas. Steep for 5–10 minutes (start with shorter amounts of time for milder teas). Here are some of our favorite herbal blends:

Calming Tea

½ teaspoon dried chamomile
½ teaspoon dried holy basil (tulsi)
½ teaspoon dried lemon balm

Tummy Tea

½ teaspoon dried peppermint leaves
½ teaspoon dried fennel seeds, lightly crushed
½ teaspoon dried marshmallow root
(*Althaea officinalis*)
Optional: ¹⁄₁₆ teaspoon ground ginger or two thin-sliced pieces of fresh ginger

Detox Tea

½ teaspoon dried dandelion (all parts)
½ teaspoon dried burdock root
½ teaspoon dried chicory root

Cognition Tea

½ teaspoon dried sage or dried rosemary
½ teaspoon dried hibiscus flowers
(not for pregnant animals)
½ teaspoon turmeric powder
Optional: 1 cinnamon stick

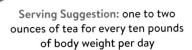

Serving Suggestion: one to two ounces of tea for every ten pounds of body weight per day

TUMMY TEA
TONIC

DETOX
TEA TONIC

CALMING TE
TONIC

COGNITION
TEA TONIC

We also love these dandelion teas, suggested by Rita Hogan, Canine Herbalist:

Fresh Dandelion Leaf or Flower Tea

8 ounces water

2 tablespoons fresh dandelion
leaves or flowers

Bring water to a near boil.
Add dandelions.
Steep for 5–10 minutes.

Dried Dandelion Leaf or Flower Tea

8 ounces water

1½ tablespoons dried dandelion
leaves or flowers

Bring water to a near boil.
Add dandelions.
Steep for 10–15 minutes.

Fresh Dandelion Root Tea

2 cups water

2 tablespoons fresh dandelion root, chopped

Bring water to a boil.
Add dandelion roots.
Lower heat and simmer for 30 minutes.

Dried Dandelion Root Tea

2 cups water

1 tablespoon dried dandelion root, chopped

Bring water to a boil in a pan.
Add dandelion roots.
Lower heat and simmer for 30 minutes.

Serving Suggestions:
Leaf or Flower Tea: ¼ cup for every ten pounds
Root Tea: ⅛ cup for every ten pounds
Give twice daily over food.

COMPLETE
and
BALANCED
MEALS

Making your own dog or cat food is the ultimate way to know *exactly* what your beloved is eating. You know what day the food was made, what ingredients you used, and, most important, that they're getting top-notch nutrition.

Our recommendation has been—and will always be—to feed as much fresh food as your schedule and budget allow. Whether you decide to make all your pet's meals, or just keep some backup meals in the freezer, we've made these recipes as flexible as possible, offering dozens of nutritionally complete meal options with endless possibilities for nutrient diversification. You can use these complete and balanced recipes as meal toppers to supercharge dry food, mix them in as part of your animals' daily food intake, feed a fresh meal a few times a week, or completely switch to all fresh food. No matter what you choose, our goal is to inspire you in the kitchen and give your pet nourishing, home-cooked meals they will love.

How Our Complete and Balanced Recipes Are Different

The number one reason veterinarians dissuade pet owners from feeding homemade diets is that most people do not follow well-formulated recipes that ensure their animals consume the daily minimum (and preferably optimal) nutritional requirements. Our complete and balanced recipes meet pets' needs, complying with both US and European pet food nutrition requirements (except where noted in adult feline diets, to minimize iodine and phosphorus levels).

Our goal is to provide straightforward and easy-to-follow meals that can be fed gently cooked, raw, supplemented, and using whole foods (meaning specific food ingredients take the place of vitamin and mineral supplements). We also offer many fruit and veggie combinations, not to overwhelm you, but to inspire you! The more nutritional diversity you can introduce to your animal's bowl, the healthier their gut and body will be. Here's the proof: researchers from the landmark American Gut Project discovered that individuals who consume more than thirty plant foods per week have a more diverse microbiome than those who eat fewer than ten. (Just remember to introduce new foods at a pace that doesn't cause gastrointestinal stress.)

The nutritionally complete and balanced meals in these pages are different than other homemade recipes you may have followed because they're formulated for various activity levels. For example, a highly active ten-pound dog needs more calories than a sedentary, inactive ten-pound dog—but not more vitamins and minerals. Our recipes also account for life stages, including recipes for the specific growth phases of puppies and kittens. We want to provide the ideal nutrition for pets at *all* stages of their lives. However, we know that printing all four hundred–plus variations of these recipes isn't possible or even needed, so many recipes are available at our website. If you love the look of a certain recipe, but it's formulated for puppies and you have an inactive couch potato senior dog or a cat, you can visit www.foreverrecipes.com to find the recipe variation that's right for your pet.

Scan this code or visit **www.foreverrecipes.com** to unlock over 400 variations of the complete and balanced meals featured in this chapter.

SCAN ME

How the Recipes and Feeding Instructions Were Formulated

You can skip this part unless you're into geeky formulation details.

These recipes meet the latest criteria for recommended allowances from FEDIAF. These recommended allowances are for growing and adult dogs and cats, meet a metabolic basis for specific activity levels and calorie consumption, and do not exceed extrapolated FEDIAF maximum nutrient requirements on a metabolic basis per day.

The formulation software we used to create these recipes is the ADF, which combines USDA and verified international food data to build a comprehensive nutritional database of ingredients, in collaboration with practicing veterinarians, board-certified veterinary nutritionists, pet food producers, and other industry professionals using up-to-date FEDIAF and AAFCO (Association of American Feed Control Officials) guidelines. We used 2021 FEDIAF guidelines for these recipes. All recipes also meet 2021 AAFCO guidelines, excluding phosphorus for adult cats (opting for FEDIAF's lower requirements). We used the lowest iodine requirements (AAFCO) for all adult cat recipes.

All recipes were formulated in Atwater, on a caloric basis (not dry matter), using the following metabolic multipliers (K factors): 110 for adult dogs, 85 for less active dogs. Puppy feeding directions based on NRC 2006, page 38–39 and Table 15–2, using K factors of 210 (early growth), 175 (mid growth), and 140 (late growth). Cat and kitten feeding instructions based on FEDIAF table VII-9, VII-10. Cat K factors: 52 (less active), 75 (indoor adult), 100 (outdoor adult), 169 (kitten early growth), 141 (kitten mid growth), 113 (kitten late growth). Nutrient losses during cooking were accounted for using USDA retention values. To see more formulation details, visit www.foreverdog.com.

Feeding for Life Stages and Activity Levels

Our life stage categories include Canine Growth, Adult Canine, Adult Canine Less Active, Kitten Growth, Adult Cat, and Adult Cat Less Active. To determine which recipes to feed your pet, choose which life stage and activity level best suits your pet:

- **Canine Growth** recipes are formulated to meet the nutritional requirements of puppies (immature dogs that are still growing). Our growth diets are appropriate for all breeds, including large and giant breed puppies. You'll alter the amount of food you feed to your puppy during early, mid, and late growth phases to account for their ongoing development, as noted in the feeding instructions found on page 157.

- **Adult Canine** recipes are best suited for dogs that get 1–3 hours of daily, active movement. Examples include brisk walks for at least an hour a day, jogging or hiking with a human several times a week, ongoing interaction/play with another dog or kids in the house, being outside several hours a day in cold climates, and digging or fence-running for part of the day. Follow "Active Dog" feeding instructions. If you have a *highly* active dog (one that spends all day moving and running), use Active Adult Dog recipes and "Active Dog" feeding instructions, and if needed, increase the amount you feed to maintain a healthy body condition.

- **Adult Canine Less Active** recipes are for dogs that get less than an hour of exercise a day (i.e., slow walks around the neighborhood), are sedentary, or are older and prefer resting to being active around the house and backyard. Less active adult dog owners should follow the "Less Active" feeding instructions.

- **Kitten Growth** recipes meet the nutritional requirements of kittens (immature cats that are still growing) and are appropriate for all breeds. You'll alter the amount of food you feed to your kitten during early, mid, and late growth phases to account for their ongoing development, as noted in the feeding instructions on page 157.

- **Adult Cat** recipes meet European standards for phosphorus and US standards for iodine. Because adult cats do best with the lowest intake of these minerals over time, we chose the lowest minimum requirements for both. If you have an outdoor cat or an active indoor/outdoor cat, follow the Adult Cat recipes and use the "Adult Cat, Outdoor" feeding instructions, and if needed, increase the amount you feed to maintain a healthy body condition during colder months.

- **Adult Cats Less Active** get less than an hour of engaged play or exercise a day. These cats may also be older and prefer resting or sleeping most of the day. Follow the "Less Active" feeding instructions.

A Pound of Feathers vs. a Pound of Bricks: Each recipe contains ingredients that have different calories and weigh different amounts, which is why the volume of food you'll give your pet is different for each recipe. You'll only need to calculate the amount to feed your animal once, per recipe, unless their activity level or weight changes.

Karen met Susan Recker on the first day of veterinary school in 1993, and they've been best friends ever since. Susan was instrumental in creating the diversified themes and food profiles in the Complete and Balanced recipes. Dr. Recker's lifelong loves are family, animals, and food (she's a fantastic chef). She believes food can be powerful medicine, and her ability to create delicious and nutritious meal plans and recipes has been invaluable to her clients and patients (as well as her friends and family). In addition to working as a small animal clinician and in academia, she also helps veterinarians learn how to formulate nutritionally complete diets using the Animal Diet Formulator (ADF), arguably the most extensive international food ingredient database and comprehensive pet food formulation tool in the world.

Steve Brown has been formulating nutritionally complete meat-based dog and cat foods for thirty years, and he played a central role in creating these recipes. In 1999, he introduced a new pet food category to the US market: nutritionally balanced, minimally processed fresh food diets, which has quickly become one of the fastest-growing segments of the pet food industry. He went on to develop the Animal Diet Formulator, or ADF, which we used to formulate these recipes.

How Much Food Should I Feed my Pet?

To calculate how much food to feed per day, follow these steps:

1. Determine what life stage and activity category they fit into (see page 155).

2. Weigh them.

3. Refer to the following Feeding Instruction Charts to see how many calories they need per day.

4. Write that number down and save it.

5. When you make a Complete and Balanced recipe, notice that it lists the number of calories per ounce. To calculate how many ounces of food to feed your pet, divide the calories your animal needs per day by the number of calories per ounce of food. For example, a less active thirty-pound (13.6kg) dog needs 603 calories a day, according to the chart. The Argentinian Beef with Chimichurri recipe contains 44 calories per ounce.

603 ÷ 44 calories = 13.7 ounces of food per day

6. Spread those ounces and calories across a day. For most pets, that will be 1–2 meals per day, and for puppies, it may be 3. Many cats like to eat their calories over 6–8 smaller meals.

APPROXIMATE CALORIC REQUIREMENTS FOR ADULT CANINES, BASED ON ACTIVITY LEVEL

ADULT CANINE, LESS ACTIVE

Canine weight, lbs	Canine weight, kg	Calories per day
3	1.4	107
5	2.3	157
10	4.5	264
15	6.8	358
20	9.1	445
30	13.6	603
40	18.2	748
60	27.2	1014
80	36.3	1260
100	45.4	1490
120	54.5	1700

ADULT CANINE, ACTIVE

Canine weight, lbs	Canine weight, kg	Calories per day
3	1.4	139
5	2.3	203
10	4.5	342
15	6.8	464
20	9.1	575
30	13.6	780
40	18.2	968
60	27.2	1312
80	36.3	1625
100	45.4	1925
120	54.5	2200

APPROXIMATE CALORIC REQUIREMENTS FOR PUPPIES, BASED ON GROWTH AND DEVELOPMENT

PUPPY, EARLY GROWTH

(Less Than 50 Percent of Adult Weight)

Puppy weight, lbs	Puppy weight, kg	Calories per day
1	0.45	116
3	1.4	265
5	2.3	388
10	4.5	653
15	6.8	885
20	9.1	1098
30	13.6	1490
40	18.2	1847
60	27.2	2500
80	36.3	3100
100	45.4	3675
120	54.5	4200

PUPPY, MID GROWTH

(50–80 Percent of Adult Weight)

Puppy weight, lbs	Puppy weight, kg	Calories per day
1	0.45	97
3	1.4	221
5	2.3	324
10	4.5	544
15	6.8	738
20	9.1	915
30	13.6	1240
40	18.2	1540
60	27.2	2090
80	36.3	2590
100	45.4	3060
120	54.5	3500

PUPPY, LATE GROWTH

(80+ Percent of Adult Weight)

Puppy weight, lbs	Puppy weight, kg	Calories per day
1	0.45	77
3	1.4	177
5	2.3	259
10	4.5	435
15	6.8	590
20	9.1	732
30	13.6	933
40	18.2	1232
60	27.2	1670
80	36.3	2070
100	45.4	2450
120	54.5	2800

APPROXIMATE CALORIES PER DAY NEEDED FOR ADULT CATS, BASED ON ACTIVITY LEVEL

ADULT CAT, INDOOR
(Less Active)

Cat weight, lbs	Cat weight, kg	Calories per day
3	1.4	64
5	2.3	90
7	3.2	113
9	4.1	134
11	5.0	153
13	5.9	171
15	6.8	188
18	8.2	213

ADULT CAT, INDOOR
(Active)

Cat weight, lbs	Cat weight, kg	Calories per day
3	1.4	92
5	2.3	130
7	3.2	163
9	4.1	193
11	5.0	220
13	5.9	247
15	6.8	271
18	8.2	305

ADULT CAT, OUTDOOR
(Highly Active)

Cat weight, lbs	Cat weight, kg	Calories per day
3	1.4	123
5	2.3	173
7	3.2	217
9	4.1	257
11	5.0	294
13	5.9	329
15	6.8	362
18	8.2	410

APPROXIMATE CALORIC REQUIREMENTS FOR KITTENS, BASED ON GROWTH AND DEVELOPMENT

KITTEN, EARLY GROWTH
(Up to 4 Months)

Kitten weight, lbs	Kitten weight, kg	Calories per day
1	0.45	100
3	1.4	208
5	2.3	293
7	3.2	366
9	4.1	434
11	5.0	496
15	6.8	610

KITTEN, MID GROWTH
(4–9 Months)

Kitten weight, lbs	Kitten weight, kg	Calories per day
1	0.45	82
3	1.4	173
5	2.3	244
7	3.2	305
9	4.1	360
11	5.0	413
15	6.8	510

KITTEN, LATE GROWTH
(9–12 Months)

Kitten weight, lbs	Kitten weight, kg	Calories per day
1	0.45	66
3	1.4	138
5	2.3	195
7	3.2	244
9	4.1	290
11	5.0	330
15	6.8	407

Weigh your animals monthly to make sure you are feeding the correct amount of food. Overweight animals that are dieting should be weighed weekly until the desired weight is achieved. Know that they can safely lose 1–2 percent of their body weight per month—but no more than 0.5 percent of their body weight per week.

Finally, always weigh food on your food scale, in ounces. If you want to transfer the weighed volume into measuring cups (or your favorite scoop), do so after you've measured accurately on a food scale. Do you feed your pet two meals a day? Split the per day amount in half and divide it between meals. Want to use part of the meal in lick mats or an interactive toy? Start with the volume of food needed for a day and divide as you like!

How to Change Your Animal's Main Meals

To avoid GI upset, you should gradually introduce new diets to your animals rather than all at once. To plan for this, consider: How much fresh food do you ultimately want to add to your pet's bowl—daily or a few times a week? You don't have to have an answer immediately. Once you start adding fresh food to your pet's diet, you may find it so easy you can step it up and add it more often.

To make the transition seamless, follow these steps:

- **Step 1:** Make one of the complete and balanced meal recipes in this book. If your animal has a sensitive stomach, choose a homemade recipe that has a similar protein to what their current food is (if they are currently eating a beef diet, choose a homemade beef recipe).

- **Step 2:** Replace 10 percent of current food with 10 percent new, homemade food. Mix very well. Monitor poop. Some cats and finicky dogs may need to start with a smaller amount, maybe a 5 percent swap.

- **Step 3:** Continue to replace 10 percent old food with 10 percent new food until you are feeding as much new, homemade food as you wish to feed.

Notes on Specific Ingredients

While most of the ingredients in our recipes are straightforward—such as beef, eggs, herbs, mushrooms, and vegetables—many ingredients may require you to travel beyond the grocery store. We include these because they provide key whole food nutrition for your pet. Fear not: we are not asking you to forage for wild plants or source exotic ingredients from specialty markets. You may have to visit your health food stores or shop online, however, and here's why.

- **Bonemeal:** Growing dogs and cats need calcium and phosphorus supplied in their food, yet many supplements contain other vitamins and minerals (like human doses of vitamin D and copper) that can be unsafe for pets. We remedied these issues by choosing the calcium and phosphorus source Mother Nature provides for dogs and cats: bones. Human-grade bonemeal is sterilized to eliminate the risks of potential zoonotic diseases, can be third-party verified for contaminants (purity tested), and is easy to find at local health food stores or online. Do not use bonemeal powder from a garden center, as it's not approved for consumption (and hasn't been contaminant tested). Look for bonemeal powder that's 28–30 percent calcium and 12–13 percent phosphorus with no other additions.

- **Eggshell Powder:** Many adult recipes do not require supplemental phosphorus, so DIY eggshell powder (calcium carbonate) works perfectly, and a recipe is on page 52. You can swap a commercial calcium carbonate supplement (same volume as eggshell powder) if you don't want to make your own.

- **Nutritional Yeast:** Nutritional yeast provides vitamins B1, B2, B6, and B12. It's also a rich source of beta-glucans, a soluble fiber that's especially beneficial for the immune system and has anti-tumor and anti-obesity activity, as well as bone regenerative properties. Nutritional yeast is different from baker's or brewer's yeast in that it's been inactivated, so it's no longer viable (or capable of replication). For this reason, it's also incapable of causing yeast issues in pets.

- **Fish Oil:** When recipes call for added fish oil, it's intended to meet your animal's DHA and EPA omega-3 requirements. You can use whatever EPA/DHA source you wish (see page 27 for suggestions).

More on Bonemeal vs. Raw Bones: Many seasoned raw feeders choose whole ground (and unground) carcasses, but because edible raw bones aren't for all dogs and cats, we settled on supplements to meet calcium and phosphorus requirements. Never feed any type of cooked bones to pets under any circumstances.

More on Calcium Carbonate: Calcium carbonate is one of the most popular forms of human calcium supplementation because it contains the highest amount of elemental calcium (around 40 percent by weight), compared to calcium citrate (just over 20 percent calcium). This results in much less volume of calcium powder per recipe if calcium carbonate is used. It's also the cheapest form of calcium. The criticism of calcium carbonate is that strong stomach acid is needed for optimal absorption, which suits a carnivore perfectly because they naturally have very acidic stomachs, so they take in this form of calcium just fine.

Can I Swap Out or Skip Ingredients? We don't recommend it. Exchanging or eliminating ingredients alters the nutritional profile of the recipe, potentially creating imbalances. The smallest volume of herbs or other add-ins have been included to provide specific nutrients or health benefits that are important. You can find complete nutritional profiles for all the recipes at www.foreverdog .com.

Note, however, that in several recipes, we've indicated substitutions you can make while keeping the recipe complete and balanced. The recipe yield and calories per ounce still corresponds to the original ingredients. For calorie information when using the substitutions, visit www.foreverdog.com.

You may also wonder why certain ingredients appear in many recipes, or why we chose what we did. Specifically:

- **Eggs:** Eggs are used as a rich source of required choline and bioavailable amino acids. Decreasing the number of eggs in the recipe will likely result in choline deficiency.

- **Herbs and spices:** Herbs and spices are used to meet some trace mineral requirements, especially manganese and magnesium.

- **Oysters:** Oysters are used to meet zinc requirements. Canned oysters packed in water are easy to find in grocery stores. If you want to swap with a zinc supplement, 1 ounce of oysters = 10 milligrams of zinc supplement.

- **Salt:** Salt is a required mineral necessary for electrolyte balance that must be provided in the diet. Plain table salt is fine to use in these recipes, although many brands are enriched with iodine, which isn't ideal for adult cats who don't need iodine supplementation, long-term. We prefer Himalayan (pink) salt because it's more mineral-dense, with no added anticaking agents.

Food Prep for Complete and Balanced Meals

Some of you may be old pros in the kitchen, while others may not remember where you keep the knives. These recipes require minimal prep work, so you don't need any special culinary skills. For the most part, the basics of human food prep apply to pet food prep as well.

For instance, chopping, mincing, dicing, or shredding ingredients can be done by hand or in a food processor or blender. A food processor is the fastest way to mince, but note that the more potent ingredients—like raw ginger, turmeric, garlic, cranberries, and fresh herbs—need to be fine to ensure the potent tastes, polyphenols, and flavonoids can be evenly distributed. Therefore, they may require a few extra spins in the processor.

Grind or finely chop meat to an almost smooth consistency for cats, very small dogs, or finicky animals. Larger dogs tend to accept more coarsely chopped meats mixed with finely chopped or pureed produce. As your animals adapt to eating homemade meals they may enjoy and seek out more chunky meats, veggies, and fruits. Obviously, animals with no teeth need the smallest food particle sizes, with many guardians blending the

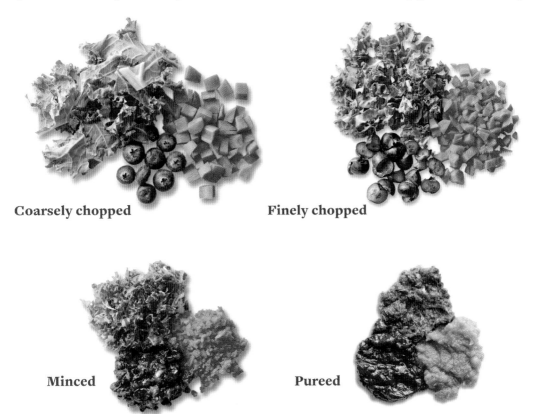

Coarsely chopped   **Finely chopped**

Minced   **Pureed**

food to the consistency of a thick puree for easier swallowing. The rule of thumb is you shouldn't see undigested food in your animal's poop. If you see identifiable food in the stool, whiz up the ingredients to be smaller in the next batch, and you may need to add a few teaspoons of water or broth if you choose to use a blender.

All of our recipes are formulated to be served either raw or gently cooked, using the lowest heat and retaining moisture. A slow cooker (Crock-Pot) is ideal, but poaching in a covered pot on the stovetop works, too. If you'd like to bake your pet's food, refer to www.foreverrecipes.com for the formulation that accounts for greater nutrient loss in the oven. Other DIY recipes you may have followed don't always account for nutrient losses due to cooking methods, but we do.

The whole food ingredients listed in our recipes are raw (except if you buy canned salmon), but feel free to use thawed-from-frozen meats, fish, fruits, and veggies. Likewise, anywhere sardines, oysters, or mussels are included, these can be fresh, raw, frozen, cooked, or canned.

Understanding Ground Meat Labels: Unfortunately, many meat labels do not indicate the meat's fat percentage, but using the correct meat leanness is a main determiner of whether or not any recipe is complete and balanced. Therefore, you have to calculate leanness as follows:

- Look at grams of fat in a serving size.
- Divide fat grams by serving size.

12 fat grams ÷ 100-gram serving size = .12 = 12 percent fat

Defining "Complete and Balanced": Dogs and cats need certain vitamins and minerals supplied in adequate amounts from the food they eat for the food to be considered "nutritionally complete," yet pet multivitamins and whole food supplements such as spirulina or phytoplankton are grossly insufficient in providing adequate amounts in appropriate quantities. Our recipes ensure that all nutritional needs are completely met.

The term "balanced" is a little trickier to explain because there's no singular definition accepted by NRC, AAFCO, and FEDIAF. Our definition relates to the relationship of nutrients to one another (for example, the ratio of calcium to phosphorus) as well as volume of nutrients consumed. "Balanced" foods should not exceed safe upper limits of nutrient tolerances (as extrapolated by FEDIAF), provide macronutrients (protein, fat, moisture, and fiber) in the ballpark of a dog and cat's evolutionary or ancestral diet, and meet FEDIAF's Recommended Allowances (RA) of nutrients, based on an animal's metabolic needs.

How to Prepare the Vitamin and Mineral Supplements in Supplemented Recipes

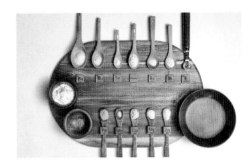

In the book and at www.foreverrecipes.com, you'll see two types of recipes incorporating either mostly whole foods or using vitamin and mineral supplements. Using supplements reduces the cost of making homemade food, but it still requires prep work. If you choose a recipe that calls for supplements, open the number of capsules needed and pour the powder contents of all the supplements into a separate dish. Discard empty capsules. If you are using supplements in pill or tablet form, crush to a fine powder with a mortar and pestle. Add bonemeal, kelp, or eggshell powder with all of the other supplements listed and mix well, then add half the vitamin and mineral powder to the bowl of food, dusting the powder evenly over the entire bowl. Mix well, add the remaining half, and mix again. It's imperative the powders are mixed thoroughly and completely into the entire batch of food, so that the added nutrients are distributed evenly throughout. For this reason, sourcing dry vitamin and mineral supplements (versus liquid or gelcaps) from your local health food store or online is recommended.

Again, if you see a recipe on the following pages that is made with supplements, you can visit www.foreverrecipes .com and find the whole foods version. And if you find a whole foods recipe and would prefer to make it with supplements, the same holds true.

Four Ways to Cook (or Not Cook) Complete and Balanced Meals

How long you decide to cook your animal's food is totally up to you and your goals. It is completely fine to serve all food raw, but you may not want to, and we've accounted for that. If your goal is to kill any potentially pathogenic bacteria, once the meat achieves an inner temperature of 165°F (use a meat thermometer to determine this) you've accomplished your goal and can remove the food from the heat source. If your goal is to make the veggies softer because your dog has a tender mouth and needs soft foods, use a fork to check for desired consistency, and remove the food from heat immediately after achieving it. You may opt to cook your veggies al dente (tender but firm) and blend with raw or partially cooked meat, or vice versa, add minced raw veggies to fully cooked meat. It's fine to cook both the meat and veggies or cook nothing. Sometimes, animals that have eaten raw food their whole lives decide they no longer want their food raw, when they're older. These cooking methods provide you with safe, nutritious alternatives, and if you need tips to feed picky or hesitant eaters, see page 34.

Raw: All these recipes can be served entirely raw. If you have concerns about potential parasites, place all meat and fish in the freezer for three weeks after purchasing (which kills tapeworms, roundworms, flukes, and flatworms). If you want to feed raw veggies with cooked meats, poach or slow-cook the meat, then add it to the rest of your raw meal.

Poached, stovetop: This is how you make recipes into delicious, mouthwatering stews (canned food consistency). To poach, make the recipe as directed and then add to a large pan, cover food with filtered water, and cover the pan with a lid. Simmer on low heat until internal temperature reaches 165°F. Serve and store with any leftover cooking liquid, as it's full of nutrients. For visual instructions on how to poach, see the recipe for "Whitefish, Lamb, and Egg Supreme" on page 226.

Crock-Pot/slow cooker: To "gently cook" recipes, add mixed ingredients to a Crock-Pot/slow cooker set to low heat, with no water added. Cook to desired doneness and serve with any nutrient-filled liquid that's run off. Cooking duration varies, depending on ingredients and the size of your Crock-Pot, so check on the cooking process regularly when making a recipe for the first time.

Baked: Baked recipes can be found at www.foreverrecipes.com. They are their own formulations that account for more nutrient loss than occurs with the gentle cooking in a slow cooker or stovetop poaching. Baked meals should be cooked in a dish that has a secure lid and on the lowest heat setting for your oven. Bake in covered cookware until desired doneness. Baking at higher heat or uncovered will result in more AGE formation and nutrient depletion. Check on the cooking process regularly when making a recipe for the first time.

Finally, a word on AGEs (see also page 68). While the best way to limit AGEs in food is to serve meals raw, poaching and gently cooking are second best. In addition, when you cover food with a lid during cooking, you dramatically reduce moisture loss, which reduces AGEs and preserves nutrients. We don't recommend other pet food cooking methods on a routine basis (frying, broiling, grilling, smoking, etc.) because they create substantially more AGEs or other unwanted tagalongs and have more nutrient loss.

Cooking for Picky Eaters: We find that finicky animals, pets that don't feel well, or hesitant eaters often prefer gently cooked foods first. That's because cooked food releases a tantalizing aroma that can stimulate appetite.

Storing, Freezing, Thawing, and Reheating

You may want to make big batches of food, and it's fine to double or triple the volume of recipes if you're feeding many mouths, big mouths, or want to prepare food less often. All recipes can be frozen for future feeding.

We recommend feeding all frozen food within one month to avoid nutrient losses over time, and you should thaw food in the refrigerator, then feed within three days. Don't refreeze thawed food. Use common sense and store and thaw raw meat products separately from other foods.

If your freezer food develops "freezer burn," the grayish discoloration that occurs when frozen food is exposed to air, your food is still safe, but it's lost some nutritional content. We recommend rotating in some fresh food to serve along with the previously frozen food.

Throw out foods that smell spoiled. Sanitize your counters, cutting boards, and utensils, and wash your hands after preparing or serving raw food. Don't leave raw food meals out more than two hours, and wash bowls after feeding.

If your animal prefers gently warmed food, heat thawed food in a hot water bath, double boiler style. This means you should place your pet's container of food into a larger container of hot water, then allow it to heat up. Avoid the microwave, as it heats food unevenly.

A Note on Photos: We've included photos with each complete and balanced recipe. You should note that each photo highlights the main ingredients in each recipe. However, photos do not depict actual volumes of ingredients needed—and some photos don't depict all the ingredients needed. Follow a specified recipe exactly—*not* the photo—when making homemade pet food.

Basic Beef and Broccoli

We've limited our first recipe to a few ingredients to show you how easy it is to create complete and balanced meals. Both versions translate to the same nutritional intake in terms of vitamins and minerals.

Adult Canine, Whole Foods
Yields 5¾ pounds
44 calories/ounce

48 ounces (3 pounds) ground beef, 90 percent lean

16 ounces fresh broccoli

6 large eggs, shelled

8 ounces cooked salmon

6 ounces beef liver

2 ounces raw sunflower seeds

25 grams wheat germ oil

8 grams ground ginger

8 grams ground cloves

5 grams nutritional yeast

17 grams eggshell powder

2 grams kelp powder (containing 700 micrograms of iodine per gram of kelp powder. This is a total of 1,400 micrograms iodine if you choose to use an iodine supplement instead of kelp powder.)

1. In a large bowl, mix food ingredients (except eggshell and kelp powders) together.

2. In a small bowl, mix powders together, stirring well.

3. Dust ½ the powder over food and mix very thoroughly. Add remaining powder and mix thoroughly again.

4. Serve raw, poached, or gently cooked.

Adult Canine, with Supplements
Yields 4½ pounds
50 calories/ounce

48 ounces (3 pounds) ground beef, 90 percent lean

16 ounces fresh broccoli

6 ounces beef liver

2 ounces raw sunflower seeds

2 grams salt

Supplements

- 11 grams calcium carbonate
- 1,400 micrograms iodine
- 300 milligrams magnesium
- 2,500 milligrams choline
- 10 grams fish oil with at least 250 milligrams EPA+DHA per gram, without added vitamin D
- 8 milligrams manganese
- 50 milligrams thiamine (vitamin B1)
- 1,000 IU vitamin D
- 100 IU vitamin E

1. In a large bowl, mix food ingredients together.

2. In a small bowl, mix supplements together, stirring well.

3. Dust ½ the powder over food and mix very thoroughly. Add remaining powder and mix thoroughly again.

4. Serve raw, poached, or gently cooked.

Balanced
with
Whole
Foods

Balanced
with
Supplements

Vit
D
Vitamin D

Vit
B4
Choline

Vit
E
Vitamin E

Vit
B1
thiamine

53
I
Iodine
126.90447

20
Ca
Calcium
40.078

25
Mn
Manganese
54.938045

15
P
Phosphorus
30.973762

12
Mg
Magnesium
24.3050

Garden-Fresh Goodness

Garden-Fresh Goodness is a sumptuous salad of green for your pet's bowl, rich in vitamin C from red peppers, fiber and antioxidants from cucumbers, and one of our favorite Forever Foods, sardines, for a dose of omega-3s and CoQ10. We've added arugula, also known as rocket, because it packs in a punch of beta-carotene, prebiotic fiber, and vitamin K, and its high alpha lipoic acids address oxidative stress. Even if your pet usually turns their nose up at arugula, you may find it blends in well with the other flavors here. If not, feel free to substitute with any green, leafy vegetable.

Adult Canine, Whole Foods
Yields 6 pounds
45 calories/ounce

50 ounces (approximately 3.125 pounds) ground beef, 90 percent lean

8 large eggs, shelled

6 ounces beef liver

6 ounces canned sardines packed in water, drained

6 ounces arugula

5 ounces cucumber with peel

5 ounces sweet red pepper

3 ounces raw sunflower seeds

8 grams dried parsley

8 grams dried basil

8 grams celery seed

8 grams dried tarragon

25 grams wheat germ oil (or 100 IU vitamin E supplement)

5 grams nutritional yeast

15 grams eggshell powder

2.5 grams kelp powder (containing 700 micrograms of iodine per gram of kelp powder. This is a total of 1,750 micrograms iodine if you choose to use an iodine supplement instead of kelp powder.)

1. In a large bowl, mix food ingredients (except eggshell and kelp powders) together.

2. In a small bowl, mix powders together, stirring well.

3. Dust ½ the powder over food and mix very thoroughly. Add remaining powder and mix thoroughly again.

4. Serve raw, poached, or gently cooked.

Kelp Is Complicated: Kelp is Mother Nature's iodine supplement. There is *huge* variability in iodine content of kelp powder, so buy a brand that lists 700 micrograms of iodine per gram of kelp powder. Alternatively, you can substitute an iodine supplement for kelp, as directed in the recipes. Our recipes have been formulated to meet your pet's iodine requirements to a T, including metabolic adjustments for cats (for more on why iodine is so important, see page 189).

Beef Bourguignon with Mussels

With tender chunks of beef in a hearty stew of tomatoes, mushrooms, and carrots, Beef Bourguignon is one of the most beloved traditional dishes of France. The human version calls for red wine, but we've substituted beef liver to add a rich, stick-to-the-ribs flavor (and meet copper requirements). Instead of pearl onions (found in the human version but toxic to dogs) we've sprinkled in mussels, a rich source of omega-3s and vitamin D. Vive la France!

Adult Canine, Whole Foods

Yields 5¼ pounds

42 calories/ounce

50 ounces (approximately 3.125 pounds) ground beef, 90 percent lean

8 large eggs, shelled

6 ounces beef liver

8 ounces mussels (or 6 ounces cooked salmon), or substitute 500 IU vitamin D + 50 milligrams magnesium + 2 grams fish oil with at least 250 milligrams EPA+DHA per gram

5 ounces mushrooms (any type)

5 ounces fresh tomatoes

5 ounces carrots

2 ounces raw sunflower seeds

8 grams ground cloves

25 grams wheat germ oil (or 100 IU vitamin E supplement)

8 grams dried thyme

8 grams dried parsley

5 grams nutritional yeast

2 grams kelp powder (containing 700 micrograms of iodine per gram of kelp powder. This is a total of 1,400 micrograms iodine if you choose to use an iodine supplement instead of kelp powder.)

15 grams eggshell powder

1. In a large bowl, mix food ingredients (except kelp and eggshell powders) together.

2. In a small bowl, mix powders together, stirring well.

3. Dust ½ the powder over food and mix very thoroughly. Add remaining powder and mix thoroughly again.

4. Serve raw, poached, or gently cooked.

Choline Is Crucial: We can't stress enough how important it is to maintain adequate choline levels in your diet. Choline is needed to make acetylcholine, a neurotransmitter that is essential for cognitive function. Choline also reduces homocysteine levels, which is associated with less inflammation and better cell function. **If you can't feed whole eggs, in this recipe, substitute 500 IU vitamin D and 700 milligrams choline supplement.**

Beef Mexican Fiesta

We head to Mexico for a rich dish full of flavor (thanks to cilantro) and prebiotic fiber and vitamin C (thanks to jicama). Also known as a yam bean or "the Mexican turnip," you can use jicama as part of recipes like this or as a crunchy training treat. Just be sure to peel off the skin, as it can harbor toxic mold.

Adult Canine, Whole Foods
Yields 6 pounds
44 calories/ounce

50 ounces (approximately 3.125 pounds) ground beef, 90 percent lean

7 large eggs, shelled

10 ounces raw jicama, peeled

6 ounces beef liver

6 ounces canned sardines packed in water, drained

4 ounces avocado

3 ounces raw sunflower seeds

2 ounces fresh cilantro

15 grams wheat germ oil (or 50 IU vitamin E supplement)

9 grams ground cloves

8 grams ground cumin

8 grams ground coriander

5 grams nutritional yeast

15 grams eggshell powder

2 grams kelp powder (containing 700 micrograms of iodine per gram of kelp powder. This is a total of 1,400 micrograms iodine if you choose to use an iodine supplement instead of kelp.)

1. In a large bowl, mix food ingredients (except eggshell and kelp powders) together.

2. In a small bowl, mix powders together, stirring well.

3. Dust ½ the powder over food and mix very thoroughly. Add remaining powder and mix thoroughly again.

4. Serve raw, poached, or gently cooked.

Why Wheat Germ Oil? Vitamin E is essential for skin and coat health, and wheat germ oil is one of nature's easiest ways to rapidly increase systemic vitamin E levels. **If you can't use wheat germ oil in the recipe, you can use a vitamin E supplement instead. Substitute: 15 grams wheat germ oil = 50 IU vitamin E supplement.**

Argentinian Beef with Chimichurri

For over three hundred years, gauchos have let their cattle herds graze on the wild, green grasses of the Pampas, creating more sustainable—and delicious—meat. When it's dinnertime, family chefs top cuts of beef with chimichurri, a sauce made with herbs that's the perfect topper for your animal friend's meals, too. Here, we mix it in with organ meat, salmon, and oysters for a complete and balanced meal your dog can enjoy.

Canine Growth, Whole Foods
Yields 6½ pounds
42 calories/ounce

50 ounces (approximately 3.125 pounds) ground beef, 90 percent lean

6 ounces beef liver

6 ounces cooked salmon

8 large eggs, shelled

3.5 ounces raw sunflower seeds

3 ounces beef spleen (or 36-milligram iron supplement)

3 ounces oysters (or 30-milligram zinc supplement)

11 grams ground cloves

25 grams wheat germ oil (or substitute 100 IU vitamin E supplement)

5 grams salt

2 grams nutritional yeast

8 ounces winter squash (acorn, carnival, green kabocha, buttercup, or any variety except butternut)

8 ounces summer squash (green or yellow zucchini, luffa, chayote, or others)

2 ounces fresh parsley

15 grams dried oregano

2.5 grams kelp powder (containing 700 micrograms of iodine per gram. This is a total of 1,750 micrograms iodine if you choose to use an iodine supplement instead of kelp powder.)

44 grams bonemeal

1. In a large bowl, mix food ingredients (except kelp and bonemeal) together.

2. In a small bowl, mix powders together, stirring well.

3. Dust ½ the powder over food and mix very thoroughly. Add remaining powder and mix thoroughly again.

4. Serve raw, poached, or gently cooked.

Oysters for Zinc: Oysters are a naturally rich source of taurine, vitamin B12, and—crucially here—zinc. Zinc is vital for healthy skin and thyroid and immune health, yet many homemade diets are deficient. Zinc can be found in prey's teeth, testicles, and hair (all great sources of zinc, but also too gross for many folks!). Canned, aquaculture-raised oysters are not only less expensive, but—according to research—contain around 50 percent fewer microplastics than the wild-caught varieties. **If you can't find canned oysters to meet your animal's zinc requirements, substitute with a zinc supplement, which we've suggested in this recipe. 1 ounce of oysters = 10 milligrams of zinc supplement.**

Fe
26
Iron
55.845

Mn
25
Manganese
54.938045

Zn
30
Zinc
65.38

B4
Vit
Choline

California Beef

Avocados and oranges may be two of California's best-loved fruits, but the Golden State is home to 80 percent of the country's strawberry crops. Not only are strawberries a sweet, tasty treat for dogs, but they're rich in flavonoids, anti-oxidants, and fisetin, which combat oxidative stress and inflammation.

Canine Growth, with Supplements
Yields 5¼ pounds
46 calories/ounce

50 ounces (approximately 3.125 pounds) ground beef, 90 percent lean

6 ounces beef liver

6 ounces cooked salmon

6 ounces avocado

6 ounces fresh strawberries

4 ounces alfalfa sprouts

3½ ounces raw sunflower seeds

6 grams salt

5 grams nutritional yeast

42 grams bonemeal

2.5 grams kelp powder (containing 700 micrograms of iodine per gram. This is a total of 1,750 micrograms iodine if you choose to use an iodine supplement instead of kelp powder.)

Supplements

- 1,500 milligrams choline
- 100 IU vitamin E
- 54 milligrams iron
- 30 milligrams zinc
- 8 milligrams manganese

1. In a large bowl, mix food ingredients (except bonemeal and kelp) together.

2. In a small bowl, mix bonemeal, kelp, and supplements together, stirring well.

3. Dust ½ the powder over food and mix very thoroughly. Add remaining powder and mix thoroughly again.

4. Serve raw, poached, or gently cooked.

Indian Beef

This fragrant meal mimics a *saag paneer* with spinach, providing a healthy dose of folate for cell growth and lutein for eye health and tumor suppression. Cardamom—the small green pod that gives this recipe a sweet, savory flavor—has been used for centuries to enhance digestion, but it also contains powerful anti-inflammatory compounds. Beets are one of the richest sources of betanin, which exhibits antioxidant defense mechanisms, gene-regulatory activities, and neuroprotective effects, and can help lower the production of free radicals. Beets also offer the body an abundant source of nitric oxide, which helps relax and dilate blood vessels, leading to better circulation and overall heart health.

Adult Canine Less Active, Mostly Whole Foods
Yields 6½ pounds
44 calories/ounce

50 ounces (approximately 3.125 pounds) ground beef, 90 percent lean

10 large eggs, shelled

8 ounces fresh spinach

8 ounces beetroots

6 ounces beef liver

6 ounces cooked salmon

2.5 ounces raw sunflower seeds

30 grams wheat germ oil (or 100 IU vitamin E supplement)

8 grams ground turmeric

8 grams ground cardamom seeds

8 grams nutritional yeast

4 grams ground black pepper (enhances the absorption of curcumin in the turmeric)

2 grams kelp powder (containing 700 micrograms of iodine per gram. This is a total of 1,400 micrograms iodine if you choose to use an iodine supplement rather than kelp powder.)

42 grams bonemeal

Supplements

- 1,000 milligrams choline
- 100 milligrams magnesium
- 30 milligrams zinc

1. In a large bowl, mix food ingredients (except kelp and bonemeal) together.

2. In a small bowl, mix supplements, kelp, and bonemeal together, stirring well.

3. Dust ½ the powder over food and mix very thoroughly. Add remaining powder and mix thoroughly again.

4. Serve raw, poached, or gently cooked.

Yeast Power: Nutritional yeast is a whole food supplement loaded with glutathione, fiber, potassium, and—crucially in these recipes—thiamine. Thiamine, also known as vitamin B1, is vital for your pet's ability to metabolize glucose into energy. It also supports brain function and DNA production, and, without sufficient quantities, dogs and cats may experience vomiting, lethargy, or nervous system damage. Cats require two to four times more thiamine in their diets than dogs, and nutritional yeast is the best source of it. **If you can't feed your pet nutritional yeast, substitute a thiamine (B1) supplement: 1 oz nutritional yeast = 20 milligrams thiamine (vitamin B1) supplement.**

Beef Spring Flavors

In Italy, the start of spring means one thing: it's asparagus season. From Piedmont to the heel of the boot, farmers park in grocery store lots—with hand-painted signs reading ASPARAGI!—selling thin stalks of the beloved vegetable out of the backs of their trucks. Rich in prebiotic fiber, folate, vitamin K, and the flavonoid rutin, asparagus has even been shown to improve glucose metabolism, not to mention its above-average glutathione content. It's spring! Celebrate the season with asparagus.

Adult Canine Less Active, with Supplements
Yields 5¾ pounds
42 calories/ounce

50 ounces (approximately 3.125 pounds) ground beef, 90 percent lean

6 large eggs, shelled

8 ounces asparagus

6 ounces beef liver

6 ounces salmon

5 ounces green peas

3 ounces fennel bulb

2.5 ounces raw sunflower seeds

17 grams eggshell powder

Supplements

- 1,350 micrograms iodine
- 1,500 milligrams choline
- 300 milligrams magnesium
- 15 milligrams zinc
- 8 milligrams manganese
- 50 milligrams thiamine (vitamin B1)
- 100 IU vitamin E

1. In a large bowl, mix food ingredients (except eggshell powder) together.

2. In a small bowl, mix eggshell powder and supplements together, stirring well.

3. Dust ½ the powder over food and mix very thoroughly. Add remaining powder and mix thoroughly again.

4. Serve raw, poached, or gently cooked.

The Pea Problem: Many grain-free commercial dog foods use pea powder or pea protein powder instead of grain, but there can be a *big* problem with consuming large amounts of legumes. Legumes are full of sugar-binding proteins called lectins, sticky molecules that bind to the lining of the small intestine. If fed on a daily basis and in high amounts, lectins have the potential to tear up the digestive tract, prevent the absorption of nutrients, harm the gut microbiome, and lead to inflammatory diseases including diabetes, rheumatoid arthritis, and celiac disease. While cooked green peas provide this recipe delicious flavor, and they are fine to use as training treats, there is no need to feed dogs excessive amounts of legumes (meaning more than 10 percent of daily food intake) every day. Stick to reasonable amounts—in the form of treats, toppers, or as part of a veggie add-in.

Filipino Tinola Chicken and Beef

Tinola is a one-pot Filipino classic: a light stew consisting of meat, papaya, and greens, cooked with good-for-the-gut ginger till the ingredients are tender. We've included manganese-rich coconut cream, which has been found to help balance blood sugar levels. When your pet is feeling yucky, on a rainy day, or just because, try this nourishing, soulful recipe with a flavorful kick. *Kain tayo* (let's eat!).

Adult Canine, Mostly Whole Foods
Yields 6¾ pounds
44 calories/ounce

52 ounces (3.25 pounds) ground beef, 90 percent lean

16 ounces (1 pound) ground chicken, 14 percent fat

6 large eggs, shelled

7.5 ounces beef liver

12 ounces fresh spinach

6 ounces papaya

40 grams wheat germ oil (or 100 IU vitamin E supplement)

9 grams coconut cream, unsweetened

10 grams ground ginger

10 grams ground turmeric

5 grams ground black pepper

5 grams nutritional yeast

15 grams eggshell powder

2 grams kelp powder (containing 700 micrograms of iodine per gram kelp powder. This is a total of 1,400 micrograms iodine if you choose to use an iodine supplement rather than kelp powder.)

Supplement

- 500 IU vitamin D

1. In a large bowl, mix food ingredients (except eggshell and kelp powders) together.

2. In a small bowl, mix powders and supplement together, stirring well.

3. Dust ½ the powder over food and mix very thoroughly. Add remaining powder and mix thoroughly again.

4. Serve raw, poached, or gently cooked.

Berry Beef and Chicken Salad

This colorful creation is a fresh bowl of goodness for your pet, with one of our favorite grab-and-go training treats: berries! Berries are abundant in myricetin, a bioflavonoid that stimulates cancer cell death, including dog bone cancer cells, while the cucurbitacin found in cucumbers possesses anti-inflammatory and antioxidant properties. Use leftover berries, seeds, and cucumbers as treats after you whip together this easy summertime (or anytime) meal.

Adult Canine, Whole Foods
Yields 5¾ pounds
44 calories/ounce

36 ounces (2.25 pounds) ground beef, 90 percent lean

12 ounces (.75 pounds) chicken breast with skin

5 large eggs, shelled

8 ounces salmon

7 ounces beef liver

5 ounces cucumber with peel

5 ounces arugula, or any dark green leafy veggie

3 ounces blueberries

3 ounces raspberries

2 ounces raw pumpkin seeds

2 ounces oysters, raw or canned (or 15 milligrams zinc supplement)

25 grams wheat germ oil (or 100 IU vitamin E supplement)

10 raw, unsalted almonds

7 grams ground cloves

5 grams nutritional yeast

15 grams eggshell powder

2 grams kelp powder (containing 700 micrograms of iodine per gram. This is a total of 1,400 micrograms iodine if you choose to use an iodine supplement rather than kelp powder.)

1. In a large bowl, mix food ingredients (except eggshell and kelp powders) together.

2. In a small bowl, mix powders together, stirring well.

3. Dust ½ the powder over food and mix very thoroughly. Add remaining powder and mix thoroughly again.

4. Serve raw, poached, or gently cooked.

Beef and Chicken Forager's Delight

Animals are foragers by nature. A study of canine feces found in a late-Neolithic dwelling site in Slovenia (estimated fifth to second century BC) revealed companion dogs ate a wide variety of plant matter, likely from shrubs and growth on the ground. With mushrooms, dandelion greens, root vegetables, and essential fatty acid–rich hempseeds (which can lower liver and kidney markers—good news for pets at risk of developing chronic kidney, liver, and cardiovascular diseases), this meal is a forager's dream come true.

Adult Canine, Whole Foods
Yields 5¾ pounds
46 calories/ounce

36 ounces (2.25 pounds) ground beef, 90 percent lean

16 ounces (1 pound) ground chicken, 14 percent fat

7 large eggs, shelled

8 ounces dandelion greens

6 ounces UV-exposed mushrooms, any type (see page 47 on how to increase vitamin D levels in mushrooms by UV exposure)

6 ounces beef liver

5 ounces Jerusalem artichokes

1.5 ounces hempseeds, hulled

1 ounce oysters, canned or raw (or 10 milligrams zinc supplement)

45 grams wheat germ oil (or 100 IU vitamin E supplement)

8 grams dried parsley

8 grams dried basil

5 grams nutritional yeast

15 grams eggshell powder

1.5 grams kelp powder (containing 700 micrograms of iodine per gram, for a total of 1,050 micrograms iodine if you choose to use an iodine supplement rather than kelp powder)

1. In a large bowl, mix food ingredients (except eggshell and kelp powders) together.

2. In a small bowl, mix powders together, stirring well.

3. Dust ½ the powder over food and mix very thoroughly. Add remaining powder and mix thoroughly again.

4. Serve raw, poached, or gently cooked.

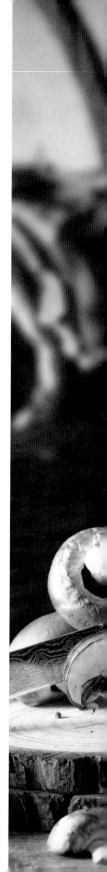

The Importance of Iodine for Dogs: Iodine is essential to your pet's metabolism and thyroid hormone production, and without sufficient intake, dogs can develop hypothyroidism. Unfortunately, compared to humans, dogs don't do a very good job of storing iodine in their bodies, which means their dietary iodine needs are higher than most pet parents may realize. (Cats store iodine remarkably well, which is why our feline recipes have far less iodine.) Most homemade dog food recipes may not provide the iodine your pet needs, so one of the best ways to supplement is by giving your dog seaweed products, including kelp. Not only is kelp rich in natural iodine, but it also contains prebiotic fibers, amino acids, and phytonutrients, including lycopene and carotene. **If you can't feed your dog kelp, substitute with an iodine supplement: 0.5 grams iodine-rich kelp powder (the specific type called for in the recipes) = 1 tablet or capsule (350 micrograms) of iodine supplement.**

Beef and Chicken Gumbo

Gumbo is the official state food of Louisiana, famous for its blend of celery, peppers, and onions, thickened into a hearty stew using okra. We skip the onions but re-create this Creole classic with a savory mix of beef, chicken, sardines, and veggies. *Laissez les bons temps rouler* (Let the good times roll)!

Adult Canine, Whole Foods
Yields 7¼ pounds
46 calories/ounce

48 ounces (3 pounds) ground beef, 90 percent lean

16 ounces (1 pound) ground chicken, 14 percent fat

9 large eggs, shelled

8 ounces fresh or canned sardines (packed in water, drained)

7 ounces beef liver

6 ounces sweet red peppers

6 ounces okra

4 ounces celery

50 grams wheat germ oil (or 200 IU vitamin E supplement)

1.5 ounces hempseed, hulled

2 ounces oysters (or 15 milligrams zinc supplement)

9 grams dried parsley

9 grams dried thyme

9 grams ground turmeric

5 grams nutritional yeast

18 grams eggshell powder

2 grams kelp powder (containing 700 micrograms of iodine per gram of kelp powder. This is a total of 1,400 micrograms iodine if you use an iodine supplement rather than kelp powder.)

1. In a large bowl, mix food ingredients (except eggshell and kelp powders) together.

2. In a small bowl, mix powders together, stirring well.

3. Dust ½ the powder over food and mix very thoroughly. Add remaining powder and mix thoroughly again.

4. Serve raw, poached, or gently cooked.

Okra Can Be Slimy: When it's cooked, okra may turn into goo. But it turns out that indigestible slime is a demulcent, a balm that soothes the intestinal tract and also has antiadhesive properties. Together, this causes bad bacteria to struggle to stick to the intestines. Okra's fiber helps bind up toxins, preventing resorption, and okra consumption also increases levels of the detoxifying enzymes glutathione, superoxide dismutase (SOD), and catalase.

Chinese Beef and Chicken Stir-Fry

Pak choi goes by many names, including bok choy or Chinese celery cabbage, and it's the small cruciferous vegetable with big nutritional benefits. A staple of Chinese-inspired cooking, pak choi contains chemical compounds called glucosinolates, which can protect against certain cancers. Its slightly bitter taste blends perfectly with ginger and oyster sauce for a savory "stir-fry" your pet will lap up.

Canine Growth, *Mostly Whole Foods*
Yields 6 pounds
43 calories/ounce

32 ounces (2 pounds) ground beef, 90 percent lean

16 ounces (1 pound) ground chicken, 14 percent fat

9 large eggs, shelled

8 ounces pak choi

6 ounces cauliflower

5 ounces beef liver

4 ounces raw or canned oysters (or 35 milligrams zinc supplement plus 2 grams fish oil plus additional gram of salt)

4 ounces beef spleen (or 54 milligrams iron supplement)

57 grams wheat germ oil (or 100 IU vitamin E supplement)

9 grams ground ginger

9 grams ground cloves

4 grams salt

4 grams nutritional yeast

45 grams bonemeal

2 grams kelp powder (containing 700 micrograms of iodine per gram of kelp powder. This is a total of 1,400 micrograms iodine if you use an iodine supplement instead of kelp powder.)

Supplement

- 250 IU vitamin D

1. In a large bowl, mix food ingredients (except bonemeal and kelp) together.

2. In a small bowl, mix powders and supplement together, stirring well.

3. Dust ½ the powder over food and mix very thoroughly. Add remaining powder and mix thoroughly again.

4. Serve raw, poached, or gently cooked.

Beef Spleen for Iron: Beef spleen may be hard to source in some locations, so be sure to check out local meat shops and butchers, farmers' markets, and co-ops. If not, you can find frozen spleen through online retailers. Just know that your sourcing efforts are worth it because, pound for pound, beef spleen contains *five times* as much iron—and thirty times as much heme iron—compared to beef liver. Iron is essential for providing oxygen to muscles and organs, and without enough, your pet can become weak and lethargic. Tuftsin and splenopentin, two peptides found in spleen, enhance immune function, stimulate white blood cells to fight against infections and cancer, and promote the growth of killer cells, which destroy sick, virus-filled cells. **If you can't find beef spleen, you can substitute it with an iron supplement: 1.5 ounces beef spleen = 18 milligrams iron supplement.**

Vit
D
Vitamin D

Beef and Chicken Gyros

For humans, there are few diets better for longevity than the Mediterranean diet, and gyros—which hail from Greece—are a Mediterranean classic. We've left out the pita (though we re-created one in the photo using the gelatin Frisbee featured on page 131) but have kept gyros' signature sauce, tzatziki, a tart blend of microbiome-building yogurt, spices, and cucumbers. Chicken also contains an abundance of omega-6 fatty acids. If you want to optimize the ratio of omega-3 fats in this recipe, add ten grams of an EPA/DHA supplement (your favorite marine or fish oil) or 6 ounces of sardines (fresh or canned, packed in water).

Canine Growth, Mostly Whole Foods
Yields 6½ pounds
39 calories/ounce

32 ounces (2 pounds) ground beef, 90 percent lean

16 ounces (1 pound) ground chicken, 14 percent fat

9 large eggs, shelled

8 ounces cucumber with peel

4 ounces plain Greek yogurt

6 ounces lettuce (any type)

5 ounces beef liver

4 ounces oysters (or 40 milligrams zinc plus one gram fish oil plus one additional gram of salt)

4 ounces fresh tomatoes

3 ounces beef spleen (or 36 milligrams iron supplement)

40 grams wheat germ oil (or 100 IU vitamin E supplement)

13 grams dried rosemary

13 grams dried oregano

14 grams dried thyme

11 grams ground cloves

4 grams salt

4 grams nutritional yeast

45 grams bonemeal

2 grams kelp powder (containing 700 micrograms of iodine per gram of kelp powder. This is a total of 1,400 micrograms iodine if you choose to use an iodine supplement rather than kelp powder.)

Supplement
- 250 IU vitamin D

1. In a large bowl, mix food ingredients (except bonemeal and kelp) together.

2. In a small bowl, mix powders and supplement together, stirring well.

3. Dust ½ the powder over food and mix very thoroughly. Add remaining powder and mix thoroughly again.

4. Serve raw, poached, or gently cooked.

Cloves Fight Inflammation: Cloves have powerful anti-inflammatory effects, and one of their bioactive components, eugenol, has beneficial antibacterial, antifungal, antioxidant, antiseptic, and anesthetic properties. Cloves must be ground and never offered whole, as they can be a choking hazard. **In this recipe, cloves are added to meet manganese requirements. If you can't include ground cloves, substitute seventeen grams of ground turmeric or two milligrams manganese supplement from the health food store.**

Ruby Red Beef and Chicken

Red cabbage, meat, beets, and pomegranates—it's a feast of ruby red! This meal is as heart-healthy as they come, with antioxidant-rich pomegranates that reduce oxidative stress in canine endothelial cells (the cells that line the blood vessels). If you have a small dog, just be sure to grind or mash up the seeds so they don't pose a choking risk.

Adult Canine Less Active, Mostly Whole Foods

Yields 4¾ pounds

49 calories/ounce

32 ounces (2 pounds) ground beef, 90 percent lean

16 ounces (1 pound) ground chicken, 14 percent fat

8 ounces beetroot

4 ounces beef liver

4 ounces red cabbage

4 ounces fresh pomegranate seeds

3 ounces raw or canned oysters (or 30 milligrams zinc supplement plus one gram salt)

2.25 ounces hempseed, hulled

35 grams wheat germ oil (or 100 IU vitamin E supplement)

8 grams ground turmeric

5 grams nutritional yeast

3 Brazil nuts

12 grams eggshell powder

8 grams bonemeal

1.5 grams kelp powder (containing 700 micrograms of iodine per gram. This is a total of 1,050 micrograms iodine if you choose to use an iodine supplement rather than kelp powder.)

Supplements

- 3,000 milligrams choline
- 1,000 IU vitamin D

1. In a large bowl, mix food ingredients (except eggshell, bonemeal, and kelp powders) together.

2. In a small bowl, mix powders and supplements together, stirring well.

3. Dust ½ the powder over food and mix very thoroughly. Add remaining powder and mix thoroughly again.

4. Serve raw, poached, or gently cooked.

Powerful Pomegranate: Feeding pomegranate improves cardiovascular, nerve, and skeletal health. That's because pomegranates are rich in punicalagins, the most potent antioxidant activity of almost all known fruits.

Beef and Chicken African Stew

This hearty stew uses sweet potatoes—a staple crop of Eastern and Central Africa—as one of its main ingredients. Full of prebiotic, good-for-the-gut fiber, sweet potatoes also contain an abundance of beta-carotene, phenolic compounds, and cancer-fighting antioxidants.

Buttery Brazil nuts—one of nature's richest sources of selenium—aid proper thyroid function, cell growth, and immune response, and a deficiency in selenium can lead to thyroid disease. Humans can eat as few as two Brazil nuts a day and receive all the selenium they need in their diets!

Adult Canine Less Active, Mostly Whole Foods
Yields 5 pounds
48 calories/ounce

32 ounces (2 pounds) ground beef, 90 percent lean

16 ounces (1 pound) ground chicken, 14 percent fat

6 ounces sweet potatoes

6 ounces fresh tomatoes

6 ounces green zucchini or yellow summer squash

5 ounces beef liver

3 ounces raw or canned oysters (or 30 milligrams zinc plus 6 milligrams iron plus 1 gram salt)

2.5 ounces hempseeds, hulled

45 grams wheat germ oil (or 100 IU vitamin E supplement)

7 grams ground ginger

7 grams ground cinnamon

5 grams nutritional yeast

1 raw Brazil nut

10 grams eggshell powder

10 grams bonemeal

1.5 grams kelp powder (containing 700 micrograms of iodine per gram. This is a total of 1,050 micrograms iodine if you choose to use an iodine supplement rather than kelp powder.)

Supplements

- 1,000 IU vitamin D
- 3,000 milligrams choline

1. In a large bowl, mix food ingredients (except eggshell, bonemeal, and kelp powders) together.

2. In a small bowl, mix powders and supplements together, stirring well.

3. Dust ½ the powder over food and mix very thoroughly. Add remaining powder and mix thoroughly again.

4. Serve raw, poached, or gently cooked.

Vit
B4
Choline

Vit
D
Vitamin D

Beef and Chicken Surf and Turf

A perfect balance of land and sea! With mussels, oysters, organ meat, beef, chicken, and delicious, nutritious fruits and vegetables, this complete and balanced recipe is a meat- and fish-based delight your beloved will devour.

Adult Cat and Adult Cat Less Active, Mostly Whole Foods
Yields 5¼ pounds
44 calories/ounce

32 ounces (2 pounds) ground beef, 90 percent lean

16 ounces (1 pound) ground chicken, 14 percent fat

13 ounces raw or canned mussels (or 495 milligrams potassium supplement plus 2 grams salt plus 50 milligrams magnesium supplement plus 4 grams fish oil containing at least 250 milligrams EPA+DHA per gram)

5 ounces mushrooms (any kind)

3 ounces zucchini or yellow summer squash

5 ounces beef liver

4 ounces beef spleen (or 36 milligrams iron supplement and 297 milligrams potassium supplement)

3 ounces chicken liver

3 ounces oysters (or 30 milligrams zinc supplement and 297 milligrams potassium supplement)

43 grams wheat germ oil (or 100 IU vitamin E)

18 grams nutritional yeast

8 grams ground turmeric

8 grams ground cinnamon

8 grams ground ginger

14 grams eggshell powder

0.75 grams kelp powder (containing 700 micrograms of iodine per gram. This is a total of 525 micrograms iodine if you choose to use an iodine supplement rather than kelp powder.)

Supplements

- 300 IU vitamin D
- 6,000 milligrams choline
- 3,000 milligrams taurine

1. In a large bowl, mix food ingredients (except eggshell and kelp powders) together.

2. In a small bowl, mix powders and supplements together, stirring well.

3. Dust ½ the powder over food and mix very thoroughly. Add remaining powder and mix thoroughly again.

4. Serve raw, poached, or gently cooked.

Meat Loaf for Everyone!

Meat loaf is classic American comfort food—for pets and their people. Here, we elevate meat loaf beyond ketchup- and egg-soaked ground beef to a nutritionally balanced meal with ground pork and salmon as its base. Throw in some spinach and you have a cancer-fighting dish your pet will devour. How does spinach fight cancer? It contains more sulfoquinovosyl diacylglycerol (SQDG) and mono-galactosyldiacylglycerol (MGDG) than any other green vegetable, and both slow cancer cell growth. This recipe can be served to both dogs and cats, young and old!

Canine and Cat, All Life Stages, with Supplements
Yields 4½ pounds
42 calories/ounce

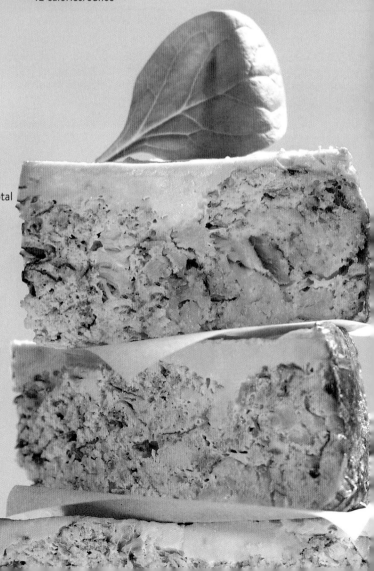

28 ounces ground pork, 12 percent fat

13 large eggs, shelled

14 ounces salmon

7 ounces raw spinach

4 grams salt

33 grams bonemeal

2 grams kelp powder (containing 700 micrograms iodine per gram of kelp powder. This is a total of 1,400 micrograms iodine if you choose to use an iodine supplement rather than kelp powder.)

Supplements

- 3,000 milligrams choline
- 3,000 milligrams taurine
- 90 milligrams iron
- 10 milligrams copper
- 75 milligrams zinc
- 200 milligrams magnesium
- 8 milligrams manganese
- 1 tablet vitamin B Complex (B50, 50 milligrams), crushed
- 100 IU vitamin E

1. In a large bowl, mix food ingredients (except bonemeal and kelp powders) together.

2. In a small bowl, mix powders and supplements together, stirring well.

3. Dust ½ the powder over food and mix very thoroughly. Add remaining powder and mix thoroughly again.

4. Serve raw, poached, or gently cooked.

Pork Hawaiian Luau

Around 300 AD, when Polynesians rowed toward Hawaii across vast stretches of the Pacific Ocean, they brought two types of animals with them: dogs and pigs. The legacy of poi dog—that now extinct breed—lives on in this recipe, which contains some of the best foods of Hawaii. One of these is bromelain-rich pineapple, which assists in digestion, calms gastrointestinal irritation, and reduces inflammation.

Adult Canine, with Supplements
Yields 5 pounds
39 calories/ounce

28 ounces pork,
12 percent fat

11 large eggs, shelled

13 ounces salmon

6 ounces carrots

6 ounces fresh pineapple

6 ounces banana

7 grams ground cloves

32 grams bonemeal

1 gram kelp powder
(containing 700 micrograms
iodine per gram of kelp
powder. This is a total of
700 micrograms iodine if
you choose to use an iodine
supplement rather than kelp
powder.)

Supplements

- 6 milligrams copper
- 45 milligrams zinc
- 18 milligrams iron
- 100 micrograms vitamin B12
- 100 IU vitamin E

1. In a large bowl, mix food ingredients (except bonemeal and kelp) together.

2. In a small bowl, mix powders and supplements together, stirring well.

3. Dust ½ the powder over food and mix very thoroughly. Add remaining powder and mix thoroughly again.

4. Serve raw, poached, or gently cooked.

Pork "Roast" with Apples

Few foods are more comforting than a well-cooked roast. We prefer not to roast meat for pets because the high heat increases AGEs and depletes many of the beneficial nutrients, so we've modified this recipe to give your pet all the flavor and *more* nutrition. At its heart is cabbage. We recommend the purple variety, which contains *four times* more antioxidants than green and has been shown to reduce the markers of gut inflammation by as much as 40 percent in cell cultures. The pectin in apples also helps balance the bowels and nourish the microbiome while preventing growth of harmful microbes. Curl up with your best friend and enjoy a slow, satisfying anti-inflammatory meal together. Family time as it should be!

Adult Canine Less Active, with Supplements
Yields 4¼ pounds
40 calories/ounce

28 ounces pork,
12 percent fat

14 ounces salmon

6 large eggs, shelled

6 ounces cabbage,
any variety

5 ounces apples, skin on

3 ounces carrots

7 grams dried rosemary

7 grams ground cinnamon

11 grams eggshell powder

2 grams kelp powder
(containing 700 micrograms
iodine per gram of kelp,
to provide a total of 1,400
micrograms of iodine if you
choose to use an iodine
supplement rather than kelp
powder)

Supplements

- 60 milligrams zinc
- 1,500 milligrams choline
- 6 milligrams copper
- 300 milligrams magnesium
- 18 milligrams iron
- 8 milligrams manganese
- 1 tablet vitamin B complex
  (B50, 50 milligrams),
  crushed
- 100 IU vitamin E

1. In a large bowl, mix food ingredients (except eggshell and kelp powders) together.

2. In a small bowl, mix powders and supplements together, stirring well.

3. Dust ½ the powder over food and mix very thoroughly. Add remaining powder and mix thoroughly again.

4. Serve raw, poached, or gently cooked.

Cranberries for Cognition: Cranberries are rich in anthocyanins and proanthocyanins, which give the berries their color and may help memory recall, neural function, and circulation of oxygen and glucose to the brain.

Pork Pumpkin Patch

Your pet can enjoy an honest-to-goodness Thanksgiving feast with this meal. Gut-soothing pumpkin, polyphenol-rich cranberries, and brain-boosting turmeric blend to make a dish that's perfect for any time of the year. Brussels sprouts are also rich in a biological component called glucosinolate, which can protect against the DNA damage that can lead to cancer. It's a crisp fall day every day with this meal!

Canine, All Life Stages, with Supplements

Yields 5¾ pounds

43 calories/ounce

28 ounces ground pork, 12 percent fat

11 large eggs, shelled

19 ounces salmon

8 ounces canned or steamed pumpkin puree (not pumpkin pie filling)

8 ounces Brussels sprouts

4 ounces raw unsalted pumpkin seeds

3 ounces raw or frozen cranberries (no sugar added)

8 grams ground turmeric

8 grams dried thyme

5 grams salt

32 grams bonemeal

8 grams eggshell powder

2 grams kelp powder (containing 700 micrograms iodine per gram of kelp, to provide a total of 1,400 micrograms of iodine if you choose to use an iodine supplement rather than kelp powder)

Supplements

- 75 milligrams zinc
- 10 milligrams copper
- 54 milligrams iron
- 1,500 milligrams choline
- 200 milligrams magnesium
- 1 tablet vitamin B complex (B50, 50 milligrams), crushed
- 100 IU vitamin E

1. In a large bowl, mix food ingredients (except bonemeal, eggshell, and kelp powders) together.

2. In a small bowl, mix powders and supplements together, stirring well.

3. Dust ½ the powder over food and mix very thoroughly. Add remaining powder and mix thoroughly again.

4. Serve raw, poached, or gently cooked.

"Rojões de Porco"—Portuguese Pork Stew

Portugal is known for its pork, especially from the famous black Iberian pig. Bobi loved any type of pork, but he preferred the finest, which means muscle meat instead of ground. This Portuguese-inspired dish captures the best of Portugal's coastal climate with one of its beloved delicacies, blending flavors together for a colorful, hearty stew.

Adult Canine Less Active, with Supplements
Yields 5½ pounds
37 calories/ounce

32 ounces (2 pounds) pork muscle meat, 95 percent lean

16 ounces raw spinach

9 ounces raw or canned sardines (packed in water)

4 large eggs, shelled

4 ounces sweet green peppers

4 ounces sweet red peppers

4 ounces fresh tomatoes

4 ounces carrots

4 ounces potatoes (with skin)

85 grams olive oil

8 grams fresh garlic

8 grams ground turmeric

12 grams eggshell powder

Supplements

- 1,125 micrograms iodine
- 8 milligrams copper
- 45 milligrams zinc
- ½ tablet vitamin B complex (B50, 50 milligrams), crushed
- 100 IU vitamin E

1. In a large bowl, mix food ingredients (except eggshell powder) together.

2. In a small bowl, mix all supplements and eggshell powder together, stirring well.

3. Dust ½ the powder over food and mix very thoroughly. Add remaining powder and mix thoroughly again.

4. Serve raw, poached, or gently cooked.

Portuguese Pork Stew
(Rojões de Porco)

pork

sardines

spinach

tomatoes

carrots

eggs

sweet green&red peppers

olive oil

eggshell

potatoes

turmeric

supplements

Zn

I

E

Cu

B₉₀

garlic

Bison Kale Hash

We love bison! While it may be harder to find in some grocery stores—and can be pricier than beef—it's low in fat, packed with B vitamins, and has a sweet, earthy flavor. Paired here with kale—which offers the body sulforaphane and indole-3-carbinol, two anticancer compounds that are released when cruciferous vegetables are chewed or chopped—your pet will savor this tasty hash.

Adult Canine, Whole Foods
Yields 6 pounds
40 calories/ounce

50 ounces (3.125 pounds) ground bison, 90 percent lean

9 large eggs, shelled

9 ounces kale

7 ounces bison liver

5 ounces green beans

5 ounces mushrooms (any type)

2 ounces raw or canned oysters (or 15 milligrams zinc + 100 milligrams magnesium supplement)

35 grams wheat germ oil (or 100 IU vitamin E supplement)

9 grams dried thyme

9 grams dried oregano

9 grams ground cinnamon

9 grams ground turmeric

9 grams ground fennel

5 grams nutritional yeast

13 grams eggshell powder

1.5 grams kelp powder (containing 700 micrograms of iodine per gram. This is a total of 1,050 micrograms iodine if you choose to use an iodine supplement rather than kelp powder.)

1. In a large bowl, mix food ingredients (except eggshell and kelp powders) together.

2. In a small bowl, mix powders together, stirring well.

3. Dust ½ the powder over food and mix very thoroughly. Add remaining powder and mix thoroughly again.

4. Serve raw, poached, or gently cooked.

Bison Buddha Bowl

Buddha bowls are all about balance. This bison-based bowl accomplishes that and more, with fiber-rich radicchio as part of its base. This leafy vegetable is a part of the chicory family, and has been found to be antiviral, antioxidant, anti-inflammation, neuroprotective, and helpful against obesity. Slow down and savor this colorful dish.

Adult Canine, Mostly Whole Foods

Yields 5¾ pounds

40 calories/ounce

50 ounces (3.125 pounds) ground bison, 90 percent lean

8 ounces radicchio

8 ounces mushrooms (any type)

4 large eggs, shelled

6 ounces bison liver

6 ounces salmon

3 ounces kiwi

2 ounces flaxseed and/or chia seeds

2 raw unsalted Brazil nuts

6 grams ground cinnamon

6 grams ground ginger

15 grams eggshell powder

1.5 grams kelp powder (containing 700 micrograms of iodine per gram, for a total of 1,050 micrograms iodine)

Supplements

- 15 milligrams zinc
- 100 IU vitamin E

1. In a large bowl, mix food ingredients (except eggshell and kelp powders) together.

2. In a small bowl, mix powders and supplements together, stirring well.

3. Dust ½ the powder over food and mix very thoroughly. Add remaining powder and mix thoroughly again.

4. Serve raw, poached, or gently cooked.

Bison Autumn Harvest

Bison liver is nutrient dense and full of minerals, as well as vitamins A, D3, K2, and E, which are hallmarks of an ancestral diet. While it may be harder to find than beef liver, it's worth it. Pair it with vegetables like butternut squash and Brussels sprouts for a complete, balanced, and colorful autumn harvest, any time of the year.

Canine Growth, Whole Foods
Yields 6¼ pounds
44 calories/ounce

50 ounces (3.125 pounds) ground bison, 90 percent lean

6 large eggs, shelled

9 ounces bison liver

6 ounces sardines packed in water, drained

6 ounces butternut squash

6 ounces Brussels sprouts

4 ounces raw or canned oysters (or substitute 45 milligrams zinc supplement)

2.5 ounces raw sunflower seeds

2 ounces fresh or frozen cranberries (no sugar added)

1 ounce beef spleen (or 18 milligrams iron supplement)

30 grams wheat germ oil (or 100 IU vitamin E supplement)

9 grams ground cinnamon

9 grams dried thyme

9 grams ground cloves

6 grams salt

3 grams nutritional yeast

44 grams bonemeal

3 grams kelp powder (containing 700 micrograms of iodine per gram. This is a total of 2,100 micrograms iodine if using an iodine supplement rather than kelp powder.)

1. In a large bowl, mix food ingredients (except bonemeal and kelp powder) together.

2. In a small bowl, mix powders together, stirring well.

3. Dust ½ the powder over food and mix very thoroughly. Add remaining powder and mix thoroughly again.

4. Serve raw, poached, or gently cooked.

Cranberries for Oral Health: Among their many benefits, cranberries slow the growth of the biofilm of *Porphyromonas gingivalis* and *Fusobacterium nucleatum*, two bacterial strains that help oral plaque form. In fact, cranberries may help inhibit plaque formation by up to 95 percent.

Bison Schnitzel with Green Beans

Schnitzel is a thin slab of tenderized meat, breaded and fried. We skip the breading and frying here and offer up our bison-based version: light on meaty flavor, yet still tender and juicy. Because of its low-fat content, bison becomes well-done fast, so be sure to keep an eye on it as it cooks—or serve raw.

Adult Canine Less Active, Mostly Whole Foods
Yields 6 pounds
44 calories/ounce

50 ounces (3.125 pounds) ground bison, 90 percent lean

6 large eggs, shelled

6 ounces bison liver

6 ounces fresh green beans

8 ounces raw or canned sardines (packed in water, drained)

5 ounces mushrooms (any type)

4 ounces raw sunflower seeds

4 ounces fresh tomatoes

3 ounces raw or canned oysters (or 30 milligrams zinc supplement + 1 gram salt)

8 grams dried parsley

8 grams ground thyme

8 grams ground ginger

5 grams nutritional yeast

20 grams eggshell powder

2 grams kelp powder (containing 700 micrograms of iodine per gram, for a total of 1,400 micrograms iodine)

Supplement

• 1,500 milligrams choline

1. In a large bowl, mix food ingredients (except eggshell and kelp powders) together.

2. In a small bowl, mix powders and supplements together, stirring well.

3. Dust ½ the powder over food and mix very thoroughly. Add remaining powder and mix thoroughly again.

4. Serve raw, poached, or gently cooked.

Mango Coconut Curry with Whitefish, Lamb, and Egg

This meal is a sweet and savory treat for pets, with mangos, coconut, and a bounty of new flavors from ginger and curry powder. Ginger is one of the richest nutritional sources of manganese, an essential nutrient that helps build collagen, strengthens ligaments and tendons, and assists with metabolism and mitochondrial function. "Whitefish" is a blanket term for many types of flaky, white fish, so choose what you like, but we love cod, tilapia, flounder, sole, halibut, snapper, catfish, haddock, and grouper.

Adult Canine, with Supplements
Yields 4¾ pounds
40 calories/ounce

25 ounces fresh whitefish

1 pound ground lamb

9 large eggs, shelled

6 ounces cauliflower

4 ounces fresh mango

4 ounces sweet red peppers

2 ounces dried, unsweetened coconut meat, flaked or shredded

1.5 ounces fresh basil

7 grams mild curry powder

7 grams ground ginger

9 grams nutritional yeast

10 grams eggshell powder

1 gram kelp powder (containing 700 micrograms of iodine per gram of kelp powder. This is a total of 700 micrograms iodine if you are using an iodine supplement rather than kelp powder.)

Supplements

- 45 milligrams zinc
- 4 milligrams copper
- 100 milligrams magnesium
- 18 milligrams iron
- 100 IU vitamin E

1. In a large bowl, mix food ingredients (except eggshell and kelp powders) together.

2. In a small bowl, mix powders and supplements together, stirring well.

3. Dust ½ the powder over food and mix very thoroughly. Add remaining powder and mix thoroughly again.

4. Serve raw, poached, or gently cooked.

Choose Your Curry: Curry powders come in mild, medium, and hot, and some contain onion powder. Look for onion-free, mild curry powder when sharing with your pets. Animal studies show curry protects against oxidative stress on the brain, heart, kidneys, and nervous system, so it's an all-around smart addition for an overall bump in organ protection.

Upgraded Shepherd's Pie with Whitefish

Also known in the United Kingdom as cottage pie, shepherd's pie is as comforting as meat loaf—but with veggies for a nutritional boost. Here, we've taken out the potatoes and minced meat—typical ingredients in shepherd's pie—and added whitefish and powerful parsnips, a cream-colored root vegetable rich in prebiotic fiber, vitamin C, and polyacetylenes, chemical compounds with anticancer benefits.

Adult Canine, with Supplements
Yields 4¼ pounds
36 calories/ounce

25 ounces fresh whitefish

1 pound ground lamb

5 large eggs, shelled

4 ounces carrots

4 ounces parsnips

4 ounces fresh or frozen peas

4 ounces fresh tomatoes

8 grams dried thyme

8 grams ground turmeric

5 grams nutritional yeast

9 grams eggshell powder

1 gram kelp powder (containing 700 micrograms of iodine per gram of kelp powder. This is a total of 700 micrograms iodine if you are using an iodine supplement rather than kelp powder.)

Supplements

- 4 milligrams copper
- 30 milligrams zinc
- 100 IU vitamin E

1. In a large bowl, mix food ingredients (except eggshell and kelp powders) together.

2. In a small bowl, mix powders and supplements together, stirring well.

3. Dust ½ the powder over food and mix very thoroughly. Add remaining powder and mix thoroughly again.

4. Serve raw, poached, or gently cooked.

Lebanese Lamb and Whitefish with Green Beans

Lebanese cuisine has evolved over time, but Mediterranean-inspired menus featuring fresh fish, chickpeas, and colorful vegetables are still staples. Here we offer a nutrient-rich meal with carrots, green beans, celery, and hempseeds. The tomatoes add some juiciness and lycopene, whose antioxidant properties can reduce the risk of chronic diseases such as cancer and heart disease, and nourish eye health.

Rodney's family comes from Lebanon, so this dish holds a special place in our hearts.

Adult Canine Less Active, with Supplements
Yields 4¾ pounds
37 calories/ounce

1.5 pounds (25 ounces) fresh whitefish

1 pound ground lamb

11 large eggs, shelled

6 ounces fresh green beans

3 ounces fresh tomatoes

3 ounces celery

3 ounces carrots

12 grams raw hulled hempseeds

8 grams ground turmeric

7 grams ground cinnamon

6 grams fresh garlic

4 grams nutritional yeast

4 grams ground black pepper

11 grams eggshell powder

1 gram kelp powder (containing 700 micrograms of iodine per gram of kelp powder. This is a total of 700 micrograms iodine if you are using an iodine supplement rather than kelp powder.)

Supplements

- 6 milligrams copper
- 45 milligrams zinc
- 200 milligrams magnesium
- 18 milligrams iron
- 100 micrograms vitamin B12
- 100 IU vitamin E

1. In a large bowl, mix food ingredients (except eggshell and kelp powders) together.

2. In a small bowl, mix powders and supplements together, stirring well.

3. Dust ½ the powder over food and mix very thoroughly. Add remaining powder and mix thoroughly again.

4. Serve raw, poached, or gently cooked.

Whitefish, Lamb, and Egg Supreme

Our least complex recipe, with only a handful of whole-food ingredients in this supplemented version. Don't let its simplicity deceive you; this meal is rich in choline from eggs, vitamin E from fiber-rich asparagus, and minerals (including selenium) from whitefish. Lamb is great for pets with allergies or food sensitivities, as it typically causes fewer reactions than beef or chicken and it's higher in omega-3s than beef because sheep convert fatty acids more effectively from the foods they eat.

Adult Cat and Adult Cat Less Active, with Supplements

Yields 4½ pounds
41 calories/ounce

22 ounces fresh whitefish

12 large eggs, shelled

18 ounces ground lamb

7 ounces asparagus

14 grams nutritional yeast

1 gram salt

10 grams eggshell powder

0.5 grams kelp powder
(containing 700 micrograms of
iodine per gram of kelp powder.
This is a total of 350 micrograms
iodine if you are using an iodine
supplement rather than kelp powder.)

Supplements

- 2,500 milligrams choline
- 60 milligrams zinc
- 2,000 milligrams taurine
- 54 milligrams iron
- 4 milligrams copper
- 100 milligrams magnesium
- 8 milligrams manganese
- 400 micrograms folic acid
- 100 IU vitamin E
- 1,485 milligrams potassium

Note: This photo series shows you a shorthand version of how to poach this recipe. For more detailed instructions on poaching, turn to page 166.

1. In a large bowl, mix food ingredients (except eggshell and kelp powders) together.

2. In a small bowl, mix powders and supplements together, stirring well.

3. Dust ½ the powder over food and mix very thoroughly. Add remaining powder and mix thoroughly again.

4. Serve raw, poached, or gently cooked.

Traditional Fish, Tomato, and Rice Stew

While we don't regularly feed our pets carb-heavy meals, rice is a staple in many cuisines around the world. If you have leftover rice, feed this stew—a traditional Portuguese dish families often share with their pets—on occasion.

Adult Canine Less Active, with Supplements
Yields 3 pounds
35 calories/ounce

24 ounces fresh whitefish

8 ounces fresh tomatoes

8 ounces carrots

8 grams fresh garlic

4 ounces cooked white rice

80 grams olive oil

20 unsalted raw almonds, crushed

15 grams bonemeal

Supplements

- ½ tablet vitamin B complex B50, (50 milligrams), crushed
- 1,000 milligrams choline
- 18 milligrams iron
- 4 milligrams copper
- 45 milligrams zinc
- 8 milligrams manganese
- 675 micrograms iodine

1. In a large bowl, mix food ingredients (except for bonemeal) together.

2. In a small bowl, mix all supplements and bonemeal powder together, stirring well.

3. Dust ½ the powder over food and mix very thoroughly. Add remaining powder and mix thoroughly again.

4. Serve raw, poached, or gently cooked.

Brazilian Chicken

This chicken dish is a delightful stew with some of the best flavors of South America: coconut, ginger, and papaya, whose enzyme papain helps break down proteins (hence the reason papaya juice is often used to tenderize meat!), aids digestion, and reduces pain and swelling.

Adult Canine, with Supplements
Yields 5½ pounds
34 calories/ounce

3 pounds dark meat chicken without skin

8 ounces kale

4 large eggs, shelled

6 ounces raw or canned sardines (packed in water)

6 ounces chicken liver

5 ounces sweet red peppers

5 ounces papaya, raw, finely chopped

2 ounces unsweetened shredded coconut meat

7 grams raw ginger (or 5 grams dried ground ginger)

7 grams ground cloves

12 grams eggshell powder

2 grams kelp powder (containing 700 micrograms of iodine per gram of kelp powder. This is a total of 1,400 micrograms iodine if you are using an iodine supplement rather than kelp powder.)

Supplements

- 75 milligrams zinc
- 4 milligrams copper
- 1,000 milligrams choline
- 50 milligrams thiamine
- 100 IU vitamin

1. In a large bowl, mix food ingredients (except eggshell and kelp powders) together.

2. In a small bowl, mix powders and supplements together, stirring well.

3. Dust ½ the powder over food and mix very thoroughly. Add remaining powder and mix thoroughly again.

4. Serve raw, poached, or gently cooked.

Most Pets Are Chickened Out: Conventionally raised chickens are mass-produced by the billions, creating cheap leftover pieces and parts the pet food industry recycles into pet food. Chicken meat is naturally high in omega-6 fatty acids and doesn't contain the anti-inflammatory omega-3s (DHA and EPA), so over time chicken can become a pro-inflammatory food. Chicken meals, in rotation with a variety of other proteins, create excellent diversity, but we don't recommend a lifetime of high-omega-6 foods for overall health.

"Canja"—Chicken Stew

Canja de galinha is a simple Portuguese and Brazilian stew made of shredded chicken, rice, and a medley of vegetables. We've substituted the rice for potatoes and used dark chicken meat, chicken breasts, *and* organ meat for a full chicken feast that's perfect for when your pet is feeling cold, tired, sick—or needs an anytime pick-me-up meal!

Adult Canine Less Active, with Supplements
Yields 5¼ pounds
37 calories/ounce

18 ounces dark meat chicken without skin

18 ounces chicken breast with skin

10 large eggs, shelled

12 ounces cooked potatoes

8 ounces chicken gizzards

8 ounces chicken hearts

28 grams bonemeal

Supplements

- 10 grams fish oil with at least 250 milligrams EPA + DHA per gram
- 900 micrograms iodine
- 3 grams cod liver oil with added vitamins A & D
- 300 milligrams magnesium
- 6 milligrams copper
- 45 milligrams zinc
- 8 milligrams manganese
- ½ tablet vitamin B complex (B50, 50 milligrams), crushed
- 100 IU vitamin E

1. In a large bowl, mix food ingredients (except bonemeal) together.

2. In a small bowl, mix bonemeal and supplements together, stirring well.

3. Dust ½ the powder over food and mix very thoroughly. Add remaining powder and mix thoroughly again.

4. Serve raw, poached, or gently cooked.

The world around us is full of many beautiful things, but much of it is toxic, with cars spewing carbon monoxide exhaust into the air and microplastics made of polyethylene and polypropylene polluting our waters. Our homes and yards may not be the safe havens we imagine them to be; we spray lawns with pesticides that target the nervous system, clean surfaces with semivolatile organic compounds that destroy the microbiome, and wrap leftovers with phthalates that disrupt the endocrine system. Our pets suffer the consequences just as we do: many dogs' daily chemical intake (including chlorpyrifos, diazinon, and cypermethrin) is 22 percent higher than recommended levels, while a household cat's may be a whopping 14–100 percent higher.

Keeping our pets safe starts with us detoxifying our homes, so in these pages we've created recipes for household cleaners, lawn care techniques, laundry detergents, home scents, first aid, and more that will keep your pet free of the thousands of potentially deadly chemicals they're bombarded with daily. We've tried to keep them as easy to make as possible, while still providing the stain-, pest-, and dirt-fighting power you're used to. All of this is backed with science and uses easy-to-find ingredients that you may already have around your house.

Here's to cultivating a Forever Pet—beyond the food bowl.

Part II

The
Forever
Home

5

INDOOR AND OUTDOOR

Recipes

Unless otherwise indicated, always follow these home-based recipes exactly. Even though all ingredients are nontoxic, and we have chosen them carefully for their many science-backed benefits, combining, substituting, or omitting ingredients may make the finished products unusable (though still likely safe). And remember: keeping your home clean, yet green, is also good for *you*, meaning more time with your beloved companion.

The cost of a green lawn and a pest-free garden is huge, and we don't mean in dollar terms. One of the most commonly used chemical pesticides—glyphosate—increases the risks of cancer, causes inflammation, disrupts hormonal function, and causes cerebral dysfunction. The harm these toxins pose to the earth is just as bad, with fertilized lawns polluting our waters, releasing nitrous oxide into the air, and depleting the nutrients in the soil.

It's time to toss the toxins and go natural, using the following recipes we suggest.

All-Purpose Cleaner

Castile soaps are made from biodegradable nut- or plant-based oils (like coconut, hemp, almond, and walnut oil), and while they contain lye (it helps create suds), lye is entirely safe when used in soaps. We would never recommend you let your pet lick or ingest lye-based soap, but if they come into contact with it, they will *not* be poisoned.

Yields approximately 1½ cups

3 drops castile soap

1 cup filtered water

½ cup rubbing alcohol (70 percent)

Optional: 2–3 drops bergamot or lemon essential oil

Mix ingredients together and add to a spray bottle.

Disinfectant Spray

The citric acid in lemons is a natural biocide, but if you don't want your house to have that lemony fresh scent, you can swap lemon rinds for thirty drops of an essential oil such as rosemary or clove oil. You can even use the two in combination (fifteen drops of each). Both rosemary and clove oil—alone and together—possess significant antimicrobial effects against the bacterial strains *Staphylococcus epidermidis*, *E. coli*, and *Candida albicans*.

Yields approximately 1¾ cup

Rinds of 6 fresh lemons (or 2–3 tablespoons of lemon juice from each lemon)

2 cups rubbing alcohol (70 percent)

Optional: 30 drops of lemon essential oil

1. Add lemon rinds to alcohol.

2. Infuse for 3 weeks in a tightly covered container to prevent evaporation.

3. Pour off liquid into spray bottle.

4. *Optional*: If you like a stronger lemon scent, add 30 drops of lemon essential oil to the bottle after infusion.

Tub/Tile/Sink Disinfecting Spray

Because bathrooms come in three types—dirty, really dirty, or really, really dirty—we've provided three variations for this tub, tile, and sink disinfecting cleaner.

Option One

This is best for light cleaning.

Yields approximately 1½ cups

6 ounces white vinegar or rubbing alcohol (70 percent)

6 ounces water

20 drops of essential oil of choice (including eucalyptus, rosemary, peppermint, lemon, lavender, or others). You can mix any combination of oils, up to 20 drops.

Mix ingredients together (do not mix vinegar and alcohol—choose one or the other) and add to a spray bottle.

Option Two

This is best for light cleaning and brightening dirty grout. Unfortunately, this mixture is not stable for long periods of time and won't be as effective if it's exposed to light or air, so it's best to make it right before cleaning.

Yields 1½ cups

6 ounces hydrogen peroxide

6 ounces water

20 drops of essential oil of choice (including eucalyptus, grapefruit seed, rosemary, peppermint, lemon, lavender, or others). You can mix any combination of oils, up to 20 drops.

1. Mix ingredients together and add to a spray bottle.

2. Spray directly on grout and let sit for a few minutes, then clean with a stiff brush.

Option Three

This recipe is best on stained surfaces.

Baking soda

Hydrogen peroxide

1. Sprinkle sink, tub, or bathroom surface with baking soda.

2. Let sit for 1–2 minutes, then scrub with a brush, sponge, or washcloth.

3. Pour a small amount of hydrogen peroxide onto cloth, sponge, or brush and continue scrubbing.

4. Let sit for 1–2 minutes (or longer for tough stains) then rinse with water.

Essential Oil Essentials: Essential oils have a wide range of attributes; some have significant antimicrobial qualities that make them great for cleaning, while others function as nature's perfume, with scents that can calm the mind. Always choose 100 percent pure, high-quality essential oils from reputable companies you trust; they should never be synthetic. Also, never apply essential oil directly to a pet's skin. If someone in your home is sensitive or allergic to essential oils, we recommend not using them.

- **Eucalyptus oil:** Can help improve seasonal allergies by reducing the severity of allergic reactions.
- **Lemon oil:** Has powerful antiviral effects.
- **Orange oil:** Effective at minimizing anxiety and stress, so it's great for freshening up laundry, sheets, towels, robes, and pillows.
- **Peppermint oil:** A natural pest repellent for indoor critters.
- **Thyme oil:** A powerful antifungal that's incredibly effective against mold growth.
- **Rosemary oil:** See page 72.
- **Clove oil:** See page 73.
- **Neem oil:** A highly effective insecticide.
- **Cedar oil:** Repels ticks.
- **Catnip oil:** See page 264.
- **Geranium oil:** A terrific mosquito repellent.

Finally, *do not* use these essential oils around pets:

- **Tea tree oil can cause reactions in cats.**
- **Pennyroyal oil can cause reactions in dogs.**

Scrub Cleaner

Use this in sinks, on countertops, or anywhere that needs a good nonabrasive scrub.

1 cup baking soda

1 cup castile soap

25–50 drops orange and/or lemon essential oil

25–50 drops rosemary and/or lemongrass essential oil

2 teaspoons vegetable glycerin

1.   Add ingredients to a jar.

2.   Mix well before using.

Stone Counter Cleaner

Use this to clean up stains—big and small—on your granite, marble, and more.

Yields approximately 2½ cups

2 cups water

½ cup rubbing alcohol

3–5 drops castile soap

Optional: ½ ounce colloidal silver

Optional: 3 drops essential oil

1.   Mix well in a spray bottle.

2.   Spray directly on the stain and wipe clean with a soft cloth.

Cats Are Canaries in a Coal Mine: A recent study looked at cats' and dogs' serum, whole blood, hair, and urine levels after exposure to common pollutants polychlorinated biphenyls, polybrominated diphenyl ethers (PBDEs), organochlorine pesticides, fungicides, organophosphorus flame retardants, and melamine. Across the board, cats' levels were higher because they can't metabolize many of these chemicals.

Floor Cleaner

Use this on tile floors to mop up stains and dust, or for general cleaning.

Yields approximately 5½ cups

4 cups water

1 cup white vinegar

½ cup rubbing alcohol
(70 percent)

Optional: 3 drops essential oil
of your choosing

Mix well in a jar or bucket and
apply to floors with a mop.
There is no need to rinse floors after cleaning.

Wood Floor Cleaner

Almost all floors are heavily colonized by bacteria, including fecal bacteria, and most floors have several strains of antibiotic-resistant bacteria. Use this on wood floors to mop up stains, dust, and—yes—nasty bacteria.

Yields approximately 5 cups

4 cups water

¼ cup white vinegar

1 teaspoon olive oil

Optional: 5 drops essential oil

Mix well in a jar or bucket and apply to floors with a mop. There is no need to rinse floors after cleaning.

Furniture Polish

Wood finishes can be delicate, so test this polish on an inconspicuous part of your furniture before you use it.

Yields just over ⅓ cup

¼ cup white vinegar

2 tablespoons olive oil

2–4 drops lemon oil

1. Mix in spray bottle or small jar.
2. Apply to wood surface with clean cloth and wipe clean.

Scented Room Spray

While our simmer pot recipes on page 252 are great for making large spaces (or even your whole house) smell terrific, this room spray fits the bill for smaller spaces or single rooms.

Yields 2 cups

1 cup water

1 cup witch hazel, 100 proof (or above) vodka,
or perfumer's alcohol

10 (or more, per your smell preference) drops essential oil
(one oil alone or any combination of lemon, lime, orange, lavender,
grapefruit, chamomile, bergamot, clary sage, rosemary, lemongrass,
ginger, marjoram, frankincense, linden blossom, or others). Karen's
favorite combo is clove, orange, and linden blossom. You can also
fill the bottle with your favorite herbs and peels.

1. Combine ingredients in spray bottle.

2. Shake well and spray.

Glass Cleaner

This glass cleaner uses vinegar, one of our favorite ingredients for green cleaning. You can also use it as a rinse aid (just add it where the rinse aid usually goes), to clean drains (pour ½ cup baking soda into your drain, then follow with 1 cup white vinegar and flush with warm water when the foaming stops), as a spray for cleaning stainless steel, and more.

Yields approximately 1½ cups

1 cup water

¼ cup white vinegar

¼ cup rubbing alcohol

Add to a spray bottle and mix well.

Laundry Detergent

Wash your pet's toys, beds, sweaters, and more with this highly effective, nontoxic detergent.

Yields 1 gallon, or approximately 64 regular loads

1 cup baking soda

¼ cup sea salt

Scant 1 gallon warm water

1 cup liquid castile soap

Optional: 25–50 drops essential oils of your choice (tea tree, lemongrass, lemon, peppermint, lavender, etc.)

1. Combine baking soda and salt in an empty gallon-sized jug.

2. Add 2 cups of warm water and swirl/shake to dissolve.

3. Add castile soap and swirl to combine.

4. Add essential oils, if using.

5. Fill jug with additional warm water until water reaches the top.

Use ¼ cup per regular-sized load.

Dryer Sheets

If you like your clothes to smell fresh when they come out of the dryer, know that the "fresh" smell your clothes soak up from conventional dryer sheets actually comes from a harmful chemical additive. If you don't smell the "fresh" scent, it's because a "masking" chemical was used to cover it up. Try these nontoxic dryer sheets instead.

½ cup white vinegar

1 cup water

15–20 drops essential oils of your choice
(orange, lemon, and lavender are good options)

1. Combine ingredients in a glass jar with a tight-fitting lid.

2. Place several washcloths or cut-up T-shirts in jar to saturate.

3. Put one cloth into each load in the dryer.

4. Once dry, place the cloth back in the jar to remoisten.

Cleaning Laundry Isn't Clean: The average American family washes eighty pounds of laundry a week, and—if they're using conventional products—the toxins from their laundry spill into the water table and move into the air. Here's a sampling of some of the harmful chemicals in laundry detergent and dryer sheets:

- **Nonylphenol ethoxylates (NPEs):** These disrupt endocrine system functioning, may harm fetal development, and may cause organ dysfunction. They've already been banned in the European Union and Canada but persist in the US.

- **Linear alkyl benzene sulfonates (LAS):** When they are produced, they release carcinogens and toxins such as benzene into the environment. There is evidence they may also promote the growth of colon cancer cells.

- **1,4-dioxane:** This is a solvent that may irritate the skin, eyes, and respiratory tract, as well as cause damage to the liver and kidneys. It's now considered by scientists to be a contaminant of real concern due to its prevalence in groundwater, but, unfortunately, cleaning it up is difficult due to its chemical properties.

Fabric Deodorizer

Stinky clothes, sheets, furniture, or towels you don't have time to wash? Skip the store-bought sprays (they're toxic) and try this. Bonus! This recipe also works great as an ant deterrent and bug spray. Just don't use this on granite, stone, or houseplants because the vinegar can cause damage.

Yields approximately 1 cup

1 cup white vinegar

5 drops essential oils (We like lemon, rosemary, lemongrass, or lavender.
If you like a stronger scent, add more drops.)

Optional: Instead of essential oils, you can infuse vinegar with citrus peels and herbs. Add as many as you like, depending on your scent preferences.

To use as a spray:

1. Pour vinegar into a new mister or spray bottle.

2. Add essential oils, herbs, or peels. *Note*: If you are using peels or herbs, fill a glass quart jar halfway with peels and/or herbs. Pour vinegar into jar and let steep for 8–10 days. Then strain out peels or herbs and pour into bottle.

3. Shake well and spray.

To use as a room deodorizer:

Fill bowl with white vinegar and essential oils or infused vinegar. Place bowl in the room that needs freshening.

Use New Bottles: Never pour vinegar into a used or old cleaning bottle because trace amounts of the cleaner may be left behind in the plastic, and that may create harmful vapors. Always use a new bottle.

Carpet Powder Deodorizer

The most common ingredient in commercial carpet powders is perchloroethylene, a known carcinogen that can also cause cognitive and neurological impairment. When you vacuum it up, it becomes airborne and can be inhaled. If you want to freshen up your carpet, skip the toxins and try this easy-to-make powder.

Yields approximately 2 cups

2 cups baking soda

25–40 drops of your favorite essential oil, in any combination

1. Mix baking soda and essential oils in a bowl and mix with a whisk until chunks are removed.

2. Pour into a glass jar and let sit for 20 minutes.

3. Sprinkle on carpet before vacuuming.

Carpet Cleaner

Having pets and carpets means stains. Use this cleaner to clean up anything you, your pet, or your housemates get on your carpet.

Yields approximately 1¼ cups

¼ cup white vinegar

1 cup warm water

1 teaspoon clear dish soap

As needed: Baking soda
(dependent on size of area to be treated)

1. Mix vinegar, water, and soap in a spray bottle.

2. Sprinkle a generous layer of baking soda over the stain to completely cover the area.

3. Allow the baking soda to dry. Then vacuum.

4. Spray the liquid solution over the stain.

5. Use a clean, damp white cloth to blot the stain until no baking soda residue remains.

6. Rinse with warm water and blot with a cloth repeatedly until all residue is gone.

7. Repeat the above process as needed to completely remove the stain.

8. If any soap or baking soda residue remain, use a mixture of three parts water, one part white vinegar to rinse and blot.

Remember to Vacuum: We love this green carpet cleaner, but you should also vacuum any carpet in your house at least once a week to remove the dust mites, dander, cockroach allergens, pollution, mold spores, pesticides, and toxic gases that stick to carpets and settle in them. All of these increase your risk of developing mild cognitive problems, allergies and irritation, and asthma.

The American Lung Association and US Environmental Protection Agency (EPA) also recommend using a high-efficiency particulate air (HEPA) filter on your vacuum and having a professional deep clean your carpet annually.

Simmer Pot Home Scents

Commercial products used to "freshen" the home can be incredibly toxic. Sadly, Rodney knows this firsthand because the ingredients in a diffuser almost killed his dog, Shubie. Air fresheners, plug-ins, and many candles contain volatile organic compounds, including formaldehyde, petroleum distillates, limonene, esters, and alcohols. Air fresheners also contain endocrine-disrupting chemicals, and these can lead to cancer, diabetes, obesity, and metabolic syndrome. Try one of these nontoxic stovetop fragrance combinations instead, adjusting the amounts to your preference.

Morning Rise and Shine

¼ cup roasted coffee beans or dried used grounds

3–4 cinnamon sticks

1–2 vanilla beans or 1 tablespoon vanilla extract

1–2 tablespoons cardamom

Winter Holiday

½ to 1 cup fresh cranberries

1 orange, sliced, with peel

3–4 cinnamon sticks

2 sprigs rosemary

1 tablespoon whole cloves

Fall Spice

1 apple, sliced or in chunks, with peel

1 tablespoon pumpkin spice or 3–4 chunks pumpkin rind

3–4 cinnamon sticks

1 tablespoon whole cloves

2–3 teaspoons nutmeg

1 tablespoon vanilla extract or 1–2 vanilla beans

Optional: replace water with apple cider

Spring Garden

2–3 limes or lemons, sliced with peel, or rinds

1–2 sprigs rosemary or thyme

2–3 sprigs mint

1-inch piece of ginger, sliced

Optional: lavender

1. For all scents, bring a small pot of water to a soft boil (or slow boil in a Crock-Pot) and add one of the combinations above.

2. Reduce heat to simmer for 2–3 hours, allowing the aromas to fill your home. Add additional water if necessary.

DIY, Budget-Friendly Air Purifier

Indoor air pollution—particularly from the chemicals acrolein and arsenic—can lead to bladder cancer in both humans and dogs. Air purifiers with HEPA filters are more effective at cleaning indoor air pollution than any other kind of device, but they can be expensive (even up to $1,000). We love this budget-friendly option for removing dust, pollen, chemicals, smoke, dander, and more.

20-inch box fan

20x20-inch pleated white furnace/HVAC air filter (MERV-13 rating)

Clear packing tape

1. Place the air filter squarely against the back of the fan.

2. Use the packing tape to secure the filter to the fan, on all sides, making sure there are no gaps.

3. Turn on the fan.

Other Ways to Clean the Air: If you don't want to create your own air filter, there are many other ways to effectively rid the air in your home of toxins, allergens, and more.

- **Invest in a HEPA filter:** They are able to remove at least 99.97 percent of allergens down to 0.3 microns in size. (For reference, a strand of hair is 100 microns wide.) Note that a HEPA filter doesn't trap gases or microbes—only particles—and you should always look for the words "true HEPA" or "absolute HEPA," which indicate that it meets US government standards (see below).

- **Fill your house with pet-safe potted plants:** The microorganisms in potted plant soil can help remove benzene (found in petroleum-based products), trichloroethylene (found in paints, varnishes, and more), and formaldehyde (found in insulation, paper products, and *much* more). In fact, indoor plants can remove as many as 97 percent of the most toxic indoor pollutants in as little as eight hours. Having potted plants in your home can also decrease carbon monoxide levels by almost half, volatile organic compound levels by 75 percent, and particulate matter concentrations by 30 percent.

- **Open your windows:** A well-ventilated house allows gases from appliances to escape, as well as any dust, pollutants, and contaminants that have built up.

- **Use natural, nontoxic products:** When you use products with harsh ingredients, you're polluting the environment *and* the air in your own home.

- **Keep your pets, litter box, and carpet clean:** See page 251. Carpets harbor all kinds of pollutants and toxins. Litter boxes that aren't regularly cleaned can cause a buildup of ammonia fumes in your house, and the eggs from *Toxoplasma gondii* parasites in cat feces can become airborne, which can lead to the illness toxoplasmosis. Also, dogs can harbor dust, dirt, feces, bacteria, and pollutants in their hair, which they can spread into your home.

- **Add vegetables to your pet's diet:** Apiaceous vegetables, including carrots, parsley, celery, and parsnips, have been found to reduce the oxidative stress caused by acrolein, a chemical found in car exhaust and cigarette smoke. Feeding your pet these veggies may help their liver convert and excrete acrolein from the body.

PARSLEY	DILL	ANISE
petroselinum crispum	*anethum graveolens*	*pimpinella anisum*
CELERY	CILANTRO	FENNEL
apium graveolens	*coriandrum sativum*	*foeniculum vulgare*
CARROT	PARSNIP	CUMIN
daucus carota	*pastinaca sativa*	*cuminum cyminum*

Ant Spray

Got ants, and they're not ant farm pets? If you choose, you can include patchouli oil in this spray, which is more than 80 percent effective at repelling three different species of urban ants!

2 cups vinegar
(either white or apple cider vinegar will work)

1 cup water

1 tablespoon clear dish soap

15–20 drops essential oil
(peppermint, patchouli, and/or cedarwood)

1.   Mix all ingredients together and pour into a spray bottle.

2.   Shake before using.

Weed Remover

Cinnamon oil is a champion weed killer, and scientists even recommend it as a promising alternative to chemical herbicides. We love the smell, too!

Yields approximately 1 quart

1 quart white vinegar
(10–20 percent acetic acid)

1 ounce orange essential oil

½ ounce cinnamon essential oil

1. Mix together in a large spray bottle.

2. Spray weeds directly with solution in the heat of the day, in direct sunlight, preferably when temperatures are above 70°F. The solution works best when the soil is dry, so don't apply it the day rain is forecasted.

3. Keep pets off of sprayed areas until dry, as solution can be irritating to the skin when it's wet.

RECIPES
for the BODY

From their paws to their ears to their coats, pets' bodies need special attention. Most pet grooming products contain a long list of potentially irritating ingredients you can't pronounce, along with a hefty dose of synthetic fragrances. These easy recipes make grooming safer, because they're made with clean and simple ingredients.

Cat Bathing Tips: Most cats hate baths, so do a nail trim the day before a bath and have everything ready before you put your cat in the sink. Then:

- **Enlist a friend:** It's fastest if two people are involved—a holder and a washer.

- **Dilute the shampoo:** It spreads quickly through your cat's fur and rinses out faster. Add a small amount of Simple Shampoo (about ¼ cup, see page 260) and an additional 2 cups of warm water to a separate jar, then mix well.

- **Put an old towel in the bottom of the sink (cats feel safer if their feet don't slide).**

- **Make sure the water pressure coming out of the faucet sprayer is set to low-medium and the water temperature is warm, not hot.**

- **After washing, rinse well. Wrap kitty in a towel, and cuddle in a warm place until dry.**

Simple Shampoo

¼ cup pure castile soap

½ cup water

1 teaspoon melted coconut oil

1. Combine all ingredients and mix well.

2. Thoroughly wet your dog's coat, then rub the shampoo into the fur and down to the skin, avoiding the face and ears.

3. Rinse thoroughly.

Shampoo for Itchy Skin

With soothing, yeast-fighting coconut oil, inflammation-fighting geranium oil, and calming lavender oil, this shampoo is sweet relief for itchy skin.

¼ cup pure castile soap

½ cup water

1 teaspoon melted coconut oil

10 drops lavender essential oil

10 drops geranium essential oil

1. Combine all ingredients and mix well.

2. Thoroughly wet your pet's coat, then rub the shampoo into the fur and down to the skin, avoiding the face and ears.

3. Rinse thoroughly.

Try Carbonated Water: Carbonated water can also be an effective remedy for itchy skin because it increases blood flow but does not negatively affect any skin functions.

Coat Conditioner

This conditioner is moisturizing, soothing, and smells like a dream. Use it following a good shampooing.

Yields ⅓ cup

1 tablespoon melted coconut oil

1 tablespoon oil of your choosing (jojoba, argan, olive, or avocado)

1 tablespoon honey

1 tablespoon water or tea of your choice (we love rosemary)

1 tablespoon arrowroot powder

1. Combine all ingredients and mix well.

2. Apply to your dog's coat after shampooing and rinsing, avoiding the face and ears.

3. Leave on for 5–10 minutes, then rinse thoroughly.

Store in the refrigerator for up to three days.

Flea Shampoo

This all-natural shampoo is incredibly effective against fleas, but—like all flea remedies—it may not provide 100 percent coverage, so keep flea combing your pet and vacuuming daily.

Yields approximately 1½ cups

1 cup simmering water

Green tea bag

Peppermint tea bag

½ cup pure castile soap

¼ cup aloe vera gel

20 drops neem oil

Optional: 10 drops lavender or lemongrass essential oil

1. Bring water to a boil in a saucepan.

2. Steep tea in boiling water.

3. Remove tea bags and let cool.

4. Add castile soap and remaining ingredients and mix well.

5. Bathe your animal, avoiding eyes, nose, mouth, and ear canals. Lather well, working shampoo over entire body. Rinse well.

Probiotic Rinse for Itchy Pets

This rinse is a great solution for itchy, irritated pet skin. If the problem doesn't clear up, or if your pet is in distress, always see your veterinarian, as itchy skin may be a sign of an underlying condition.

Yields approximately 3 cups

½ cup plain kombucha tea

1 cup green tea

1 cup peppermint tea

½ cup witch hazel

½ tablespoon colostrum powder

1 teaspoon probiotic powder
(spore-forming/soil-based probiotic powder
is best)

1. Combine ingredients in a bowl, mixing well. Or put mixture into a spray bottle.

2. Pour or spray over your pet from the neck down. Avoid the eyes.

3. Rub into skin and towel dry. Do not rinse.

DIY Mosquito Spray

Cats love catnip (it's soothing to their skin), but mosquitoes hate it. Catnip contains nepetalactol, a chemical substance that spurs an uncomfortable sensation inside mosquitoes, thus repelling them. Use this spray on yourself or your pets anytime you go outdoors.

Yields approximately 2½ cups

1. Mix ingredients in misting spray bottle.

2. Shake before using. Mist body (not head) prior to outdoor adventures. Reapply every 2 hours while outside.

water
2 cups

lemon juice
¼ cup

vanilla extract
4 tablespoons

catnip oil
20 drops

DIY Mosquito Spray

DIY Pest Spritz

Neem oil, which comes from the neem tree (an evergreen native to India), fights insects by slowing their growth, smothering them, preventing molting, and interfering with their hormones, making it more difficult for them to reproduce. Vanilla also functions as a deterrent, and aloe vera gel emulsifies the mixture for even distribution.

Yields approximately 1¼ cups

1 teaspoon neem oil

1 teaspoon vanilla extract

1 cup witch hazel

¼ cup aloe vera gel

1. Add all ingredients to a spray bottle and shake vigorously until ingredients are mixed well.

2. Shake well prior to each use and immediately spritz over dog (avoid the eyes!).

3. Repeat every 4 hours while outdoors and make a fresh batch every 2 weeks.

Pest Hacks: One of Karen's favorite ways to safeguard her dogs against pests is to put an all-natural pest spray on bandanas so that it doesn't leave their coats stinky or sticky. Know that no matter how you treat your dog against pests, though, **you should always use a comb to check them for ticks and fleas when they come inside.** Fleas are a nuisance that can cause tapeworms or flea allergy dermatitis, and you can remove them with a flea shampoo (see page 262) or flea comb. But ticks can be life-threatening, so check behind their ears, in their paw pads, under their legs, and anywhere else that ticks like to burrow. No pesticide or natural deterrent is 100 percent effective.

Coat Refresher Skin Spray

Use this spray between baths to freshen up your pet's stinky fur.

Yields 2–3 cups, depending on optional add-ins

½ cup apple cider vinegar

½ cup green tea

1 cup distilled water

Optional:

½ cup peppermint tea

½ cup calendula tea

5 drops lavender essential oil

1. Combine ingredients and mix well.

2. Pour into a spray bottle.

3. Shake well and spritz as needed to keep the coat refreshed.

4. Store mixture in the refrigerator for up to a month.

Simple Eye Wash

Keeping your pets eyes clean is a necessary way to remove irritants and allergens. Many pets have fur that contributes to eye irritation, and they rely on us to remove the debris that collects in the corners of their eyes. Once a day, if needed, you can use a damp clean cloth, pure colloidal silver, or a wash like this to disinfect and clean out any goop that's accumulated. If your pet *still* has eye boogers, apply a tiny dab of coconut oil where crust and discharge tend to accumulate; they'll come off like a breeze tomorrow.

Yields approximately ½ cup

¼ cup organic no-tears baby shampoo

¼ cup distilled water

1. Mix ingredients in a clean jar.

2. Add 1 teaspoon to a clean moistened washcloth or disposable cotton pad to gently clean the fur around the eyes. Repeat until all debris has been removed. Finish by wiping around eyes with pure water.

Coat Refresher
Skin Spray

Ear Cleaner

Your pet's L-shaped ear canals make it hard for debris to exit—and easy for bacteria and fungi to grow, especially if the ears are moist—but this cleaner can help. Please don't use any narrow pointy tools to clean the inner ear, however, as they can rupture the eardrum. Also be aware that scratching, rubbing, redness, tilting the head in one direction, discharge, or odor can be signs of inflammation or a serious infection. Take your pet to the veterinarian if you notice any of these behaviors.

Yields approximately ⅔ cup

⅓ cup witch hazel

3 tablespoons hydrogen peroxide

1 tablespoon apple cider vinegar

1 tablespoon colloidal silver

1. Thoroughly mix ingredients in a bowl.

2. Pour over cotton rounds in a clean, dry container with a tight lid. Allow the liquid to fully saturate all the rounds.

3. Use as many rounds as needed to clean ears.

4. Use a dry cotton round when done to dry ear canal.

5. Store in a cool, dry place and make a fresh batch every week.

Toothpaste

Stinky breath—we're slamming the door on you! This toothpaste contains pomegranate extract, which has been found in studies to limit the growth of certain bacterial biofilms that are involved in the development of periodontal disease.

Yields approximately ¼ cup

1. Pour the liquid coconut oil into a small bowl, or directly into a small sealable container.

2. Add the baking soda or clay, pomegranate extract (open the capsule and empty the powder in, or if in tablet form, crush the tablet and add the powder), trace minerals, and essential oil (if using).

3. Mix well and pour into sealable container (if you haven't already done so).

4. Store tightly covered.

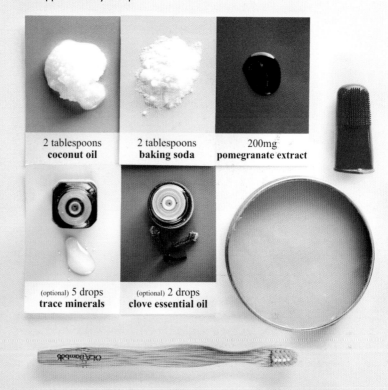

2 tablespoons **coconut oil**

2 tablespoons **baking soda**

200mg **pomegranate extract**

(optional) 5 drops **trace minerals**

(optional) 2 drops **clove essential oil**

Improve Oral Health: Poor oral hygiene is a major health risk for dogs and cats, leading to heart, kidney, and liver disease, yet at least 80 percent of dogs over three years of age have developed some form of periodontal disease. For cats, rates may be higher (some studies estimate 96 percent of cats have inflammation of the gums). Here's how to make good oral hygiene easier.

- It's important your dog or cat feels comfortable with your hands touching their mouth, so incorporate gentle facial strokes during daily cuddle time.

- Once your pet is okay with having his face and gums touched, the next step is to wrap a bit of gauze, a clean scrap of thin cotton cloth, or a cotton round around your finger, dab on a pea-sized amount of toothpaste, and rub it over teeth and gums.

- Start by brushing one tooth at a time with the gauze or cotton until all teeth are clean. Later, transition to a finger brush, then a soft pet toothbrush that's the right size for his mouth.

Dandelion Oil and Salve

Dandelion oil is liquid gold for your pet's skin! While it's been a traditional Chinese medicine and Native American remedy for thousands of years, recent studies have shown it can protect against cell damage from the sun because it decreases reactive oxidative species (ROS) activity and absorbs harmful UV rays. Use this for hot spots, cracked noses and pads, calloused elbows, cuts and abrasions, and to clean your pets' ears. You can also add this oil to an ice cube tray, freeze, and use as a medicated ice pack.

Yields depend on how many dandelion flowers you use, as well as jar size

Dandelion flower heads
(see exact measurements for salve below)

Oil (any type such as olive oil, argan oil, or coconut oil—measurements below)

1. Dry dandelion heads 24–48 hours or use dehydrator if in humid areas. They must be totally dry to avoid fungal growth.

For oil:

1. Put flower heads in jar and lightly pack. Add oil, covering all the flowers, and fill to top. Cap the jar.

2. *If you have time*: Let jar sit on a sunny, warm windowsill for 4–6 weeks. If it's in direct sunlight, cover it with a paper bag to protect it from UV rays. Strain flowers and use oil.

3. *If you have less time*: Place jar in the top of double boiler and let warm (below 110°F) for 2 hours. Strain flowers, let cool, and seal (or use).

4. *Or*: If you don't have a double boiler, place a metal ring from a mason jar in the bottom of a saucepan, then place the filled jar on top of the ring (so the jar is resting on the ring and not touching the bottom of the pan). Add enough water to cover half of the jar and warm on low heat (below 110°F) for 2 hours. Strain flowers, let cool, and seal (or use).

For salve:

1. Add ½ cup coconut oil and ⅓ cup dried dandelion flowers to a jar.

2. Place jar in the top of double boiler and let warm (below 110°F) for 2 hours.

3. Strain flowers, let cool, and seal (or use).

Paw Protector Wax

Rodney lives in Canada, so he knows how snow, ice, and sidewalk salt can damage delicate paw pads. We love this wax for its soothing, healing, and protective qualities, and we recommend using it *before* a nasty ice storm hurts your dogs' paws. It also helps repel road salt. You can pour the wax into decorative tins, muffin liners, or mason jars, tie them up with a bow, and give them as great holiday gifts for the pups in your life.

Yields about 6 ounces

1 ounce beeswax

3 tablespoons coconut oil

3 tablespoons calendula oil

3 tablespoons avocado oil

10 drops lavender essential oil

Optional: calendula flowers

1. In a saucepan, combine beeswax, coconut oil, calendula oil, and avocado oil over low heat until melted.

2. Pour into a container.

3. Add calendula flowers and essential oil and stir gently.

4. Let cool.

Paw Soak

Pets don't wear shoes, so their paws collect whatever residues and contaminants are in the environment. We love this soothing, detoxifying paw soak, especially in the evening after all outdoor walks are done. If your pooch is tiny, putting the solution in a 9x13-inch cake pan and soaking all four paws at once works well.

Yields about 1 quart

1 quart water

4 organic green tea bags

¼ cup Epsom salt

½ cup organic, raw,
unfiltered apple cider vinegar

1. Bring water to a boil, then remove from heat.

2. Add tea bags and salt, then stir well until salt is dissolved.

3. Let steep until cool.

4. Remove tea bags and add apple cider vinegar, stirring well.

5. Pour solution into a bowl that allows you to submerge one paw at a time up to your dog's wrist.

6. Allow the solution to penetrate through your dog's fur (if possible for 30 seconds).

7. Remove paw and pat dry. Do not rinse.

8. Repeat for the other 3 paws.

Pet Wipes

Colloidal silver has potent antiseptic properties, which is why many veterinarians use silver wound dressings and solutions to address a variety of external ailments, including burns, skin wounds, and skin infections. And it's face-friendly, so we love it to clean out gunky ears and around the eyes. Use these colloidal silver–based wipes on paws, ears, fur, butt, or anywhere that needs cleaning.

1 cup water

3 tablespoons colloidal silver

1 tablespoon unscented castile soap

2 tablespoons coconut oil
(above 76°F to liquefy)

Optional: 5 drops lavender essential oil

1 roll thick paper towels

1. Combine all liquid ingredients in a bowl or large measuring cup and whisk.

2. Place the paper towels, without cardboard center, in a large glass jar or a clean, recycled wipes container.

3. Pour the liquid over the paper towels to saturate.

4. Tear off one paper towel as needed.

5. Keep container tightly closed.

Acknowledgments

This book was a huge team effort and would not have come together without the people around us being so helpful and supportive during its creation.

Our awesome teammate Bea Adams worked tirelessly on this project, coordinating dozens of moving parts over many months with endless photo shoots; we could not have done this project without her. Dr. Susan Recker input endless nutrition numbers into the Animal Diet Formulator, and the ever-patient Steve Brown checked and re-checked nutrient values. We would not have completed this dream of seeing real food recipes in print without these three very committed people.

We were humbled that veterinary nutritionists Donna Raditic, DVM, DACVIM (Nutrition) and Laura Gaylord, DVM, DACVIM (Nutrition) so kindly volunteered to review recipes and nutritional profiles. Having the support of veterinarians, worldwide, that are using real food to treat and prevent real problems fed our desire to create this "how to" manual.

Dog mom Sarah Mackeigan kept Shubie well exercised, well fed, and well entertained, and our moms faithfully provided us with delicious, healthy food, day after day. Our families and the Planet Paws team did everything they could to help minimize distractions so we could focus on this creation.

Our awesome online community, Inside Scoop.pet, was well taken care of by our amazing team of admins, headed up by Renée Morin (who has remained ever faithful from the beginning). And you know your family really loves you when they volunteer to do your customer service for all incoming inquiries. Thank you, Aunt Jo.

We are grateful to our collaborator, Sarah Durand, who knew the kitchen lingo we needed, and Leah Carlson-Stanisic, who jumped in to help organize and lay out the thousands of pictures Rodney and Bea created. Finally, Kim Witherspoon, Karen Rinaldi, and Kirby Sandemeyer offered ongoing guidance throughout the project. And thank you, Ann Becker, for being our faithful family editor in chief.

Our relationships, both personal and professional, mean everything to us. We are also grateful for you, and our growing, compassionate tribe of worldwide animal advocates and pet parents who share our common goal: creating the happiest, healthiest animals possible because we know enough to make wiser choices.

Illustration Sources

All photographs by Rodney Habib and Bea Adams with the exception of the following:

Page 6: Dimitrios Karamitros; Shutterstock, Inc.

Page 7: Sarah Durand McGuigan

Page 17: Brynn Budden (Budden Designs)

Page 23: *Avocado, Rosemary, Nuts, Salmon:* Epine/Shutterstock, Inc.; *Cherries:* Nata_ Alhontess/Shutterstock, Inc.; *Garlic:* Sketch Master/Shutterstock, Inc.; *Steak:* Bodor Tividar/Shutterstock, Inc.; *Mushrooms:* Net Vector/Shutterstock, Inc.

Page 24: iStock.com/Laures

Page 29: Valeriya Bogdanovia 100/Shutterstock, Inc.

Page 31: Soloma/Shutterstock, Inc.

Pages 32: *Kiwi:* mamita/Shutterstock, Inc.; *Pea pod:* logaryphmic/Shutterstock, Inc.

Page 33: *Spinach:* Natalya Levish/Shutterstock, Inc.; *Asparagus:* mamita/Shutterstock, Inc.; *Mushroom:* Artleka_Lucky/Shutterstock, Inc.; *Tomatoes:* Olga Lobareva/Shutterstock, Inc.; *Carrots:* Vector Tradition/Shutterstock, Inc.; *Peppers:* logaryphmic/Shutterstock, Inc.; *Beans:* Nata_Alhontess/Shutterstock, Inc.; *Broccoli:* bosotochka/ Shutterstock, Inc.

Page 35: *Slippery Elm Powder, Marshmallow Root Powder:* Foxyliam/Shutterstock, Inc.; *Pumpkin:* Qualit Design/Shutterstock, Inc.; *Activated Charcoal:* Net Vector/Shutterstock, Inc.

Page 55: yoko obata/Shutterstock, Inc.

Page 58: Brynn Budden (Budden Designs)

Page 61: Brynn Budden (Budden Designs)

Page 66: macrovector/Shutterstock, Inc.

Page 68: macrovector/Shutterstock, Inc.

Page 70: *Rosemary, Cloves, Ginger, Thyme:* artnlera/Shutterstock, Inc.; *Chives:* Nata_ Alhontess/Shutterstock, Inc.; *Nutmeg:* Nikiparonak/Shutterstock, Inc.

Page 71: Oaurea/Shutterstock, Inc.

Page 79: Antonov Maxim/Shutterstock, Inc.

Page 80: mamita/Shutterstock, Inc.

Page 85: iStock.com/Gulnar Akhmedova

Page 101: *Almond, Peanut, Walnut, Cashew:* Sketch Master/Shutterstock, Inc.; *Buckwheat, Sunflower seeds:* Spicy Truffel/Shutterstock, Inc.; *Banana:* mamita/Shutterstock, Inc; *Flour:* Qualit Design/Shutterstock, Inc.

Page 112: iStock.com/PeterHermesFurian

Page 119: Rodney Habib

Page 125: iStock.com/Gulnar Akhmedova

Page 139: Kuku Ruza/Shutterstock, Inc.; VECTOR_X/Shutterstock, Inc.; Vector/ Shutterstock, Inc.

Page 145: Tatiana Kuklina/Shutterstock, Inc.

Page 149: Brynn Budden (Budden Designs)

Page 151: Brynn Budden (Budden Designs)

Page 159: Nadzeya Sharichuk/Shutterstock, Inc.

Page 162: *Egg, Salt:* Qualit Design/Shutterstock, Inc.; *Parsley:* Bodor Tirador/Shutterstock, Inc; *Oysters:* mamita/Shutterstock, Inc.

Page 171: Nikolaenko Ekaterina/Shutterstock, Inc.

Page 208: Nadezhda Nesterovia/Shutterstock, Inc.

Page 211: iStock.com/dfli

Page 241: *Chamomile:* Flaffy/Shutterstock, Inc.; *Lemon:* Irina Vaneeva/Shutterstock, Inc.; *Herbs:* Katflare/Shutterstock, Inc.

Pages 276–77: Courtesy of the family and friends of *The Forever Dog*

Index

(Page references in *italics* refer to illustrations.)

About the Authors

Veterinarian KAREN SHAW BECKER's deliberate, common-sense approach to creating vibrant health for companion animals has been embraced by millions of pet lovers around the world, making her the most followed vet on social media. She has spent her career as a small-animal clinician, empowering animal guardians to make intentional lifestyle decisions to enhance the well-being of their animals. Dr. Becker writes and lectures extensively, and serves as a wellness consultant for a variety of health-oriented organizations. She is the first veterinarian to give a TED Talk on species' appropriate nutrition, which has been a lifelong passion for her. In 2023 she received the Stange Award for outstanding professional achievement in veterinary medicine, the highest award granted by the Iowa State College of Veterinary Medicine.

RODNEY HABIB is a sought-after public speaker, filmmaker, multiple-award-winning content creator, founder of Planet Paws—the world's largest pet health page on Facebook—and, most important, a pet parent. Driven by a passion for citizen science, Habib established the nonprofit organization Paws for Change Foundation to further education and research in the area of animal nutrition and lifestyle. Habib's first TED Talk on pet health stands as the highest-viewed TED Talk in history pertaining to dogs. He was recently honored by the Canadian government as having one of the most influential platforms in Canada.

THE FOREVER DOG LIFE. Copyright © 2024 by Planet Paws Media, Inc. All rights reserved. Printed in Canada. No part of this book may be used or reproduced in any manner whatsoever without written permission except in the case of brief quotations embodied in critical articles and reviews. For information in the U.S., address HarperCollins Publishers, 195 Broadway, New York, NY 10007, U.S.A. In Canada, address HarperCollins Publishers Ltd, Bay Adelaide Centre, East Tower, 22 Adelaide Street West, 41st Floor, Toronto, Ontario, M5H 4E3, Canada.

For information, please email the Special Markets Department in the U.S. at SPsales@harpercollins.com or in Canada at HCOrder@harpercollins.com.

FIRST U.S. AND CANADIAN EDITIONS

All photographs by Rodney Habib and Bea Adams, unless otherwise noted.
Designed by Leah Carlson-Stanisic

Library of Congress Cataloging-in-Publication Data has been applied for.

Library and Archives Canada Cataloguing in Publication information is available upon request.

ISBN 978-0-06-331400-9
ISBN 978-1-4434-7004-9 (Canada pbk)

24 25 26 27 28 TC 10 9 8 7 6 5 4 3 2 1